Understanding Christian Worship

Ronald J. Wilkins

Religious Education Division
Wm. C. Brown Company Publishers
Dubuque, Iowa

To Live
Is Christ

Nihil Obstat:
Rev. William G. McLaughlin

Imprimatur:
+ James J. Byrne, S.T.D.
Archbishop of Dubuque

December 2, 1981

Editorial Consultants

for Sacred Scripture—Very Rev. Brendan McGrath, Professor of Theology, Loyola University, Chicago, Illinois; Past President, the Catholic Biblical Association of America

for Adolescent Religious Education—Mrs. Ruth Cheney, Program Services Associate for the Youth Ministry of the Episcopal Church; Chairman of the Screening Committee of the International Christian Youth Exchange

for Adolescent Psychology—Dr. William D. Wilkins, Distinguished Professor of Psychology, School of Leadership and Human Behavior, United States International University, San Diego, California; Visiting Professor San Diego University

for Social Sciences—Dr. Raymond Polin, Professor of Political Science, Graduate School, St. John's University, Jamaica, L. I.; New York

for the Canadian Provences—Mr. Leo Lewis, Consultant for the Roman Catholic School Board, Exploits—White Bay, Diocese of Grand Falls, Newfoundland, Canada

Fully aware of religious education as a key factor affecting human relations, the editors invited a Protestant and a Jewish scholar to review material presented in these two books as it bears on their respective faith communities. These are Dr. Edwin Zerin, Rabbi, and Dr. Martin E. Marty, Editor, *Christian Century.* While their personal views and religious beliefs obviously must differ from some of the views presented in these books, both feel that the content has been so handled as to increase intergroup understanding.

Book Team

Ernest T. Nedder
Publisher

Sandra J. Hirstein
Editor

Patricia C. Hail
Production Editor and Photo Researcher

Janet K. Conradi
Cover Designer

6-01802-02

ISBN 0-697-01802-4

Contents

Introduction

Technology is changing the way Americans experience the world. Space exploration and computer games take them beyond the world in which they live. Instantaneous, world-wide television, intercontinental telephones, and global telephoto communications expose them to other people's thoughts, life styles, and cultures. Medical and chemical discoveries are enabling them to live longer and more worry-free lives. Increased leisure gives them the capability to enjoy life more fully. These and other technological miracles are creating economic, political, and cultural changes at such a rate that today's realities are tomorrow's memories.

In the midst of these economic, political, and cultural changes, two things seem to remain rather constant: people's need for love and their search for an answer to the mystery of life. The need for love is satisfied in interpersonal relationships. The search for an answer to the mystery of life is experienced by most people in religious faith. Love develops from the experience of warmth and affection that an infant receives to the giving of love of truly mature people. Religious faith develops from a child's acceptance of the idea of God to the living in the presence of God of a deeply religious man or woman.

The need for love and the experience of religious faith seem to be common to the nature of human beings—though either or both may be rejected. Love is expressed in trust of another person. Religious faith is expressed in a positive relationship with whatever religious people mean by their word for God. In *Understanding Christian Worship,* we shall discuss the relationship that Catholic Christians have with their God and the way they express this relationship in their prayer and worship.

The purpose of *Understanding Christian Worship* is to help its users to come to a more mature understanding of Catholic worship. If they do, they will be able to express their relationship with God both privately and in union with other Catholics in a way that will be in keeping with their level of maturity.

The theme and tone of *Understanding Christian Worship* is expressed by the poet who, nearly 2,000 years ago, wrote in Psalm 98:

Sing a new song to the Lord;
   he has done wonderful things!

By his own power and holy
   strength
   he has won the victory.

The Lord announced his victory;
   he made his saving power
   known to the nations.

He kept his promise to the people
   of Israel
   with loyalty and constant love
   for them.

All people everywhere have seen
   the victory of our God.

Sing for joy to the Lord, all the
   earth;
   praise him with songs and
   shouts of joy!

Sing praises to the Lord!
   Play music on the harps!

Blow trumpets and horns,
   and shout for joy to the Lord,
   our king.

Roar, sea, and every creature in
    you;
    sing, earth, and all who live on
    you!

Clap your hands, you rivers;
    you hills, sing together with joy
    before the Lord,
    because he comes to rule the
    earth.

He will rule the peoples of the
    world
    with justice and fairness.

The hope of *Understanding Christian Worship* is that whoever absorbs its message will grow in love of God and express this love in the way he or she lives.

Prologue: A Call to Holiness

The Fact of Change

Have you noticed that your moods change from day to day? For example, how do you feel today as compared with yesterday? Not physically, but about things like school, your parents, your friends, and the things you like to do? Do you feel exactly like you did yesterday, or last week, or last year?

You know you don't. And that's a fascinating thing about being human. You are at once the same person and a different person. You are the same Brian, or Mary, or Nancy, or Bill as you were yesterday—or last year. But don't you experience yourself as a different Brian, or Mary, or Nancy, or Bill each day?

Don't you look at things differently and feel different about many things?

The answer, of course, is yes. But why is this so? Why are you the same person and, at the same time, a different person?

There are many reasons. One is called the dynamics of growth. This is the pattern of growth, change, and development that occurs in every human being. There is physical growth, certainly. You experience this every day in yourself and others. There is intellectual and emotional growth. You know more and feel different than you did last year or five years ago when you were a child. There is, also, social growth, spiritual growth, growth in awareness, and growth in experience. All these affect how you look

on things and how you feel about them from day to day. As you grow, so do you change.

But growth does not take place in a smooth, even way. It does not go from A to Z in a gradual incline like the hypotenuse on a triangle whose vertical side is one-fourth its horizontal side. It is, rather, like the track of a roller coaster in an amusement park with peaks and valleys, and loops and straightaways. We might wish it to be smooth, but it isn't. It might *seem* like it would be better if it were smooth, but it wouldn't be, really. Sameness is dullness. What if, for example, you always felt low—or high, for that matter. Could you stand to be always geared up or hyperactive, or always dull, listless, and disinterested?

Not only is growth not smooth, it can't be. There are just too many things involved in human growth for it to be smooth. Each aspect has its own pattern of development. Each stage has its own growth-spurt and period of adjustment to growth.

Growing to maturity is a complex process. It involves physical, mental, and emotional aspects—all acting and interacting. These in turn are affected by body chemistry, environment, personal and social interaction, and an entire range of other things which affect growth. They determine, to a large extent, how we feel about things from day to day, from one period of growth to another, and from the beginning of life to the end.

To see how your feelings about things change, compare how you feel now about the things listed below with the way you felt about them a year or so ago. After each item, put a check mark in the appropriate box on the right.

	No Change	Little Change	Some Change	Great Change
1. Going to school	☐	☐	☐	☐
2. Relationship with parents	☐	☐	☐	☐
3. Kinds of movies you like	☐	☐	☐	☐
4. Kinds of magazines you read	☐	☐	☐	☐
5. School subjects you like	☐	☐	☐	☐
6. Favorite foods	☐	☐	☐	☐
7. Sports you like	☐	☐	☐	☐
8. Sports you participate in	☐	☐	☐	☐
9. Music you like	☐	☐	☐	☐
10. Friends	☐	☐	☐	☐
11. Interest in boys/girls	☐	☐	☐	☐
12. Places you like to go	☐	☐	☐	☐
13. TV shows you watch	☐	☐	☐	☐
14. Things you do after school	☐	☐	☐	☐
15. Ambition in life	☐	☐	☐	☐

Name two things which were important to you last year which are no longer really important to you now.

Name two things which are important to you now which were not important to you last year.

Making Change Work for You

While it is true that the dynamics of growth create changing feelings about persons and things throughout life, they also create changing feelings of varying intensity and impact *within each growth period*. They affect us differently during various stages of our growth.

As you know, growth-to-maturity takes place in four general growth periods, each with its own characteristics and patterns of development. There is the infant stage, the childhood stage, the adolescent stage, and the adult stage. But do you realize that within each of these stages there are peaks and valleys of growth and development which affect how we feel about persons and things during that stage of development?

Adolescence, for example, can be defined as that period of human growth between the dependence of childhood and the independence of adulthood. It usually extends from the twelfth to the eighteenth year. But there is a big difference between a seventh grader and a twelfth grader, as you very well know. And there is a difference between what an incoming ninth grader thinks is important and what an experienced tenth grader thinks is important!

Over and above that, every adolescent of whatever age is different from every other adolescent. All have their own strengths and weaknesses, their own growth patterns, their own feelings, ambitions, and desires. They also all have their own thoughts, questions, and particular doubts.

All adolescents, it is true, exhibit most of the general characteristics of adolescence, but each exhibits them differently at different times and in different ways depending on many variables. It's no wonder then that people are pretty much the same while still so vastly different. They all go through the same stages of growth, but they all go through them differently. Everyone experiences changing feelings about persons and things, and everyone experiences changes in values and priorities.

The principal reason *you* experience *your* changing feelings about persons and things is that you are older than you were. You are not simply older physically, however. You are older intellectually and socially. Because you know more and have experienced more, you perceive things differently. Because of this, your awareness of persons and things has broadened and deepened. Their value to you has changed because your judgment about their value to you has changed.

For example, when you were much younger, you were probably excited about your first tricycle. It was important to you, and, at first, you rode it every chance you got. Then came your first bicycle and you moved out of your infant stage of life into your childhood stage. You no longer felt as you did about your tricycle. Its value to you was nil. As you moved through your childhood into your adolescence, your bicycle became less and less important, not so much because its newness had worn off but because you were older and you viewed it differently. It no longer had the same value in your eyes. If you have not yet gotten your driver's license, your passion will probably be to get one so that you will be able to drive a car. The next step is for you to own your own car—any car, just so it's your own! Having a car for yourself, or owning one is important to you. It is a value. You'll do almost anything to achieve this goal.

It's that way with so many things in life. When you were a baby, money meant nothing to you. Now it is important for what it can do for you personally. Soon it will be important for what it can do for you and for those who will depend on you for their welfare. When you were a child, your relationship with your parents was one of dependence. Now it is gradually changing and will continue to change until you will be virtually independent of them intellectually, socially, and financially.

What Is Important

But the fact of change in your feelings about persons and things, and their importance in your growth to maturity, is not what is really important here. **What is important is the kind of change taking place and the effect these changes are having on you personally and on your relationships with people with whom you come in contact.** Make no mistake about it. Change will take place whether you like it or not. The only question is, will the change be guided and controlled for good, or will it be directed, consciously or by default, away from your best interests? The answer to that question, particularly during the middle years of your adolescence, is almost entirely up

to you. Every person does determine, more or less, what he or she thinks about persons and things, how he or she feels about them, and how he or she relates to them.

At this stage of your life, it is important for you to reflect on what you think about persons and things and why you think as you do. What, for example, do you think about your parents, and why do you think as you do? From your childhood days to the present, your relationship with your parents has changed almost daily. It will continue to change as you grow older, until, perhaps, your role will be completely reversed: you may have to take almost complete charge of them and their lives. But what is your relationship with them at this moment? What is the cause (or causes, for that matter) for the state of that relationship as it now stands? Additionally, what would you like it to be?

What you think about other persons and things will also affect your relationship with them, and, by that very fact, will affect the course and tenor of your life. What, for instance, do you think about authority—about your teacher and the respect that belongs to him or her because of the role he or she plays in your life? What is your attitude about law and/or law enforcement officers? How do you feel about young children, or senior citizens? How do you get along with your grandparents if they live with you or near you? How do you feel about minority people in general or a particular minority in your neighborhood? What is the cause for the way you feel?

How do you feel about lying, stealing, cheating, destruction of property, or pollution of the environment? How do you feel about sex, abortion, euthanasia, perjury, slander and calumny, taking drugs, or drinking during high school years? How do you feel about going to church, or praying, or personal holiness? What priority do these things have in your life? More importantly, why do you feel as you do abut them?

As you stand poised on the threshold of your adult life, you may be wondering what kind of an adult life you will have. You may be searching for those things which will make your life interesting, enjoyable, profitable, and meaningful. If you are—and most middle-years adolescents do begin to think about these things—you need to search out those things that really will make your life interesting, enjoyable, profitable, and meaningful.

First, you'll need to prepare for an economically profitable job in an area of high interest for you. Then you'll need to adopt an interesting life-style which will enable you to express who you are and what your ideals are. Finally, you'll develop a philosophy of life and an expression of that philosophy which will incorporate what people over the centuries have found make human life profitable, interesting, enjoyable, and meaningful.

Examine the list of topics on the next page and after each put a plus (+) or minus (−) sign to indicate whether you now have positive or negative feelings about each. When you have done this, select three of special interest to you and be prepared to explain the reason for your present feelings.

Relationship with parents

Relationship with older brothers and sisters

Relationship with classmates

Relationship with older neighbors

Relationship with adults in general

Relationship with authority

Relationship with teachers

Relationship with priests

Relationship with minorities

Relationship with handicapped people

Relationship with the Church

Relationship with God

Slander

Pollution

Abortion

Mercy killing

Drug use

Teenage drinking

Slander

Sex

Prayer

Holiness

Going to church

Religious education

Looking at Your Changing Relationship with God

The process of changing relationships with persons and things is not only the result of growth, it is an indication of growth. Persons who cease to grow intellectually, socially, and morally stagnate. Their range of interests becomes increasingly small, and their experiences, instead of reaching out and encompassing a dynamic world, tend to repeat themselves and offer nothing new intellectually, socially, or morally.

Such a condition is fatal to human growth. The process of intellectual, social, and moral growth is like the growth of a flower or plant. When persons experience something, or many things, they assimilate them into their consciousness. They evaluate them, incorporate them into their growth process, and live with them until they experience something in addition, different, or entirely new—at which point the whole process starts over. This is what is happening to you now. You are experiencing new things physically, intellectually, and socially. You are assimilating them, incorporating what you think is important, and making them part of your "new" self.

One part of your new, or changing, self that ought to come under examination and evaluation is your changing relationship with God—your spiritual self. It is obvious to you that your relationship with God is not the same as it was when you were a child, but is it still the same as it was when you were in seventh grade? Is it the same as it was last year? Are there not some questions, doubts, or unresolved aspects about God, your prayer life, and your participation in the liturgy? Are there not ideals, desires, and, perhaps, reservations about the whole question of God and your relationship to Him that enter your mind off and on?

You have looked at your changing relationship with other persons and things that are part of your daily experience. You ought to look at your changing relationship with God. To neglect to look at your spiritual experiences and evaluate your changing relationship with God is to neglect an integral part of your total self. You are, after all, made up of several "selves"—your spiritual self is one of them. Not to look at it would stunt your growth as a person, just as the neglect of your physical self—or your intellectual, emotional, social, or moral self—would.

Like other areas of growth, spiritual growth has its peaks and valleys. There are periods of great spiritual experience, periods where we seem to be treading water, and periods of disinterest, boredom, or even of rejection. These are normal experiences of the spiritual life. Persons who do not seek out new religious awareness or new spiritual awareness cease to grow. It is entirely possible, too, that, in a "low" period, they may abandon the spiritual life altogether.

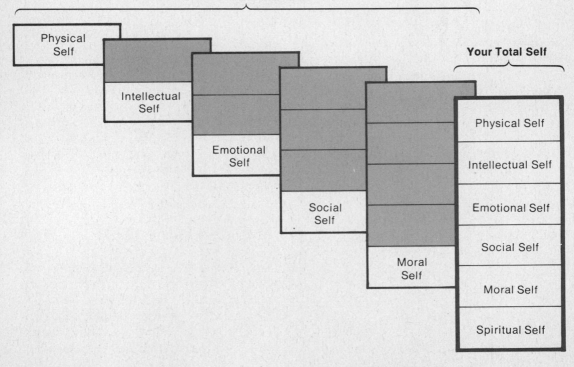

Part of Your Total Self

Physical Self

Intellectual Self

Emotional Self

Social Self

Moral Self

Your Total Self

Physical Self

Intellectual Self

Emotional Self

Social Self

Moral Self

Spiritual Self

It ought not to surprise you that at times you enjoy spiritual experiences, at times you may just be going through the motions, and at times you feel like abandoning, or do abandon, your spiritual life altogether. This is, as we have said, normal human experience. It is also God's way of helping you grow spiritually. He wants you to feel bored, perhaps, or even hostile, so that you'll say to yourself, "What am I doing?" "Why am I going to Mass?" or "Why should I pray?" so that you will examine your spiritual life and, hopefully, grow to new religious awareness, a deeper relationship with Him, and a better, stronger spiritual life.

One of the problems with examining our spiritual life, however, is that most people do not really know what is meant by "spiritual life." A person's spiritual life is not, first of all, something added to, or separate from, his or her natural life. It is, rather, part of his or her total life. It is not, secondly, a series of pious acts, prayers, or community actions totally unrelated to our secular life. Thirdly, it is not something that only "religious" people have. Everyone has a spiritual life—everyone is in some way related to God. Fourthly, it is not something that, if we "go too far," will interfere with our fun, our enjoyment of life, or our pursuit of happiness. *It is, rather, our relationship with whatever God is for us.*

Like our relationship with persons and things, our spiritual life is measured by the degree of our relationship with whatever God is for us. If we feel close to God, our degree of relationship is high. If our relationship is fairly good, our degree of relationship is fairly good. If our relationship is weak, our degree of relationship is low.

Our Call to Holiness

The term we use to describe the degree of our relationship with God is *holiness*. Like the term spiritual life, the word *holiness* is often misunderstood or completely misconceived. **Holiness, rightly understood, means the expression of the degree of our relationship with God.** That is, holiness is measured by how we relate to whatever God is for us.

Holiness, for Catholics, is expressed in the basic moral goodness of their lives—in practicing virtue instead of committing sin. It is expressed in their commitment to social justice and to works of charity. It is expressed in the nature of their personal prayer life—in how, and when, and why they pray. Finally, it is

Joy is the infallible sign of the presence of God.

expressed in the mode of their participation in the public, official acts of worship in the Church, called "the liturgy" in Roman Catholic circles.

It is a fact that many Catholics are afraid of the word "holiness." For them, it means long hours of prayer and a great deal of time spent in church. It means lives of severe penance that even the most stouthearted person would cringe from and a denial of even the most simple acts of pleasure. It means heroic deeds that they feel incapable of doing, and achievements beyond their ability. It means lives of bleakness and acts of self-denial that are too frightening to think about. It means, they think, a whole lot of things too great, too difficult, and too "impossible" for "ordinary" mortals.

Mother Teresa of Calcutta

Nothing could be further from the truth. Some of the above things may have been done by people who are holy, and some of them may have been done by people who are not so holy. These things are not holiness. Holiness, as we have said, is the degree of our relationship with God. As such it admits of degrees. Some people are holier than others, for a variety of reasons, just as some people are stronger, or smarter, or have better opportunities. But the degree of our holiness seems to depend on our understanding of Who and What our God is for us, and on our willingness to express our understanding in our actions.

You Can Be Holy

What many Catholics don't realize about holiness is that they were created to be holy. God made people so that they could share His Divine Life. Secondly, they don't realize that they are called to be holy by God Himself. "You are a chosen race," He says through His Apostle, St. Peter. "[You are] the king's priests, the holy nation, God's own people, chosen to proclaim the wonderful works of God, who called you out of darkness into his own marvelous light" (1 Peter 2: 9).

The third thing most Catholics don't realize about holiness is that they have the means to be holy. God gives them His grace, His sacraments, His acts of worship, and His call to prayer and community action to make them holy—if they choose to be so. Finally, they don't realize that they can be holy, if they try. Would God call people to holiness if it were not possible for the average human being to be holy to some degree?

11

There are lots of holy people out there. They just don't brag about it is all.

It's a funny thing about holiness. The more we try to be holy, the better persons we become! This may seem peculiar, but it is true. The better we pray, for example, the closer we come to God. The closer we come to God, the better our prayer life becomes.

The greater our participation in the liturgy, the more we reflect what the Catholic Church is, and the more people will come to know God. The more we practice virtue, the less sin we commit. The less sin there is, the better the world is for our being there. The more we become involved in acts of social justice, the better we make the lives of others. The better we make the lives of others, the more joy and goodness there is around us.

Holiness is like health. The better care we take of it, the better it becomes. In fact, holiness reflects our spiritual health.

Once you understand what holiness is, and once you realize that your spiritual life is important in making you a wholesome, well-rounded individual, you can see the importance of examining and

evaluating the nature of your own spiritual life. As we have said, because your spiritual life is an integral part of your total life, it can grow, develop, and mature until it informs your *total* life. It helps you develop a philosophy of life and a mode of living that will make your search for a happy, enjoyable, profitable, and meaningful life easier and more satisfying.

That's what you're searching for, isn't it?

Evaluate your spiritual life as it seems to you at this moment of your life by rating, on a scale of 1 to 10 (or by some other scale if you want to keep your evaluation private), each of the items listed below. When you have done this, reflect for a moment on your feelings about the condition of your spiritual life.

Do you . . .
  Feel close to God
  Feel comfortable praying
  Pray fairly often
  Feel comfortable when religion is
    discussed
  Want to know more about holiness
  Have reservations about trying to
    be holy
  Attend Mass without "having to"
  Understand the real nature of the
    sacraments
  Understand what "grace" is
  Have private spiritual devotions of
    your own
  Become aware of the presence of
    God from time to time
  Feel uneasy when God's name is
    used in a vulgar fashion

  Think of God off and on
  Want to make a retreat or day of
    recollection
  Try to lead a virtuous life
  Try to avoid deliberate, rather
    serious sin

The degree of our relationship with God is measured by our holiness.

Holiness for Catholics is expressed in a good moral life, in acts of charity, in personal prayer, and in participation in the liturgy.

Conclusion

As we have said, Christians are called to be holy. They are asked to live wholesome moral lives. They are commanded to seek for justice and to do acts of charity. They are given an opportunity to pray and to worship with their fellow Christians in the great acts of the liturgy. It is these we shall discuss in this book.

Summary

As we grow older, our relationship with persons and things changes.

Our relationship with God, too, changes as we grow older. We need to examine the state of that relationship.

Words You Should Know

Be sure that you know the meaning of the words given below. For those you are not sure of, consult the Word List on page 234.

assimilate	holiness	political
cultural	hypotenuse	priorities
complex	impact	stagnate
default	integral	technology
dynamics of growth	interacting	tenor
economics	liturgy	variables
encompass		

For Review, Discussion, Research, and Reflection

1. Why should people expect their viewpoints, attitudes, and relationships to change from time to time? Explain what causes this.

2. What things make up what your book calls "your total self"? Explain what each is.

3. Why should a person expect to have some doubts, questions, and worries about his or her relationship with God? What does your book suggest might be God's reason for this?

4. Why should a person look at the condition of his or her spiritual life from time to time? Why do you suppose most people do not?

5. Do you agree with your book's statement that people who neglect their spiritual life neglect an important part of their growth toward maturity? Why? Why not?

6. Explain what your book means by "holiness." Do you agree that everyone can be holy to a certain degree? Discuss the pros and cons of this question with your classmates.

7. What are some of the misconceptions about holiness? Why do you think people have these ideas?

8. How do Christians express holiness? Explain each briefly.

9. Read the first two chapters of The First Epistle of Peter. What is the general subject matter of these chapters? Select four verses, or phrases, which seem particularly appropriate today for achieving holiness. Does the advice of the epistle seem to urge Christians to lead "unnatural" lives? Give an example.

Part One

Expressing a Relationship with God through Prayer

Keeping in Touch
with God

You keep in touch with your friends, don't you? You go to see them, you call them on the telephone, and you go places with them. Shouldn't you at least do the same with God?

1.1 The Developing Idea of Who Our God Is

Haven't you often wondered what God is like? Most people do. After all, the problem for most people is not whether or not there is a God, but what kind of God there is. They ask themselves questions like "What (or Who) is God?" "What is God like?" "What does God do?" "Where is God, really?" "How does He affect my life?" "What should my relationship with God be like?"

To ask such questions is natural for human beings. To understand the Christian response, it is necessary to look at how Christians arrived at their understanding of Who and What God is for them.

The Christian understanding of Who or What God is, was developed only after many centuries of responses to these questions. You see, people have wondered about God for as long as they have been on earth. Primitive people believed that a Power or Force outside themselves controlled the world. They responded to this Power or Force with wonder, awe, fear, or reverence.

Age after age, people continued to ask themselves what this Power, Force, or Presence could be. Each age arrived at its own understanding, building on the expression of earlier generations. Each age added, bit by bit, to people's understanding of what God is. Even though the idea of God has developed from primitive ideas to present understanding, the central concern or principal question for each individual remains. That question is, "Who (or What) is God for me?"

The development of the idea of God kept pace with the development of people's ability to understand what they experienced. At first the idea of God was primitive and simple: the force that controlled a power of nature was a god. Because there were many powers, there were many gods. As time went on and the forces of nature were more clearly understood, relatively civilized people (10,000 to 8,000 B.C.?) began to think of their gods as superpowers residing in the heavens and controlling the universe from a "god world." Literally hundreds of "heavenly gods" populated this world, and people continued to wonder about them, fear them, pay homage to them to win their favors or put off their vengeance.

As generation succeeded generation and people became more sophisticated, so did their notions about God. While it is true that most people accepted the current ideas of God and performed the rituals associated with their beliefs, some people were uneasy about the question of God. They sought a clearer notion of Who or What God is. Eventually, those who thought seriously about God developed a better understanding of the nature of God. They progressed from the idea that all gods were somehow equal to the idea of a ranking among their gods. Eventually, the idea of a single, all-powerful god developed.

As we look back upon primitive and early civilized people's ideas of God, we are liable to dismiss them as simplistic, childish, or unreal, unworthy of the intelligence of human beings. If we do, we miss two important points about how *we* got *our* idea of God. The first is that people can know only as much as their experience lets them know. (It would be foolish to dismiss the Wright Brothers because they did not invent the 747 right

away!) Ideas develop gradually, even the idea of God. The fact that earlier generations struggled with the idea of God makes our struggle to find a God we can believe in that much easier.

The second point is that God revealed Himself gradually to people (in keeping with His developing plan for creation) *through the natural processes of people's ability to learn.* Step by step, we believe, God led people to know more of Him until they were ready to accept further ideas of God they could understand.

Our God Reveals Himself in Person

As soon as people had conceived of God as Something beyond nature, they were ready for God's new revelation of Himself. We believe that this revelation developed in two ways, both occurring about the same time, and, as usual, gradually.

The first way was *philosophically*. People began to think more logically about the question of God and sought for answers that would tell them Who or What God is.

When we say "people" we do not mean every single person, of course. We mean people in general. A few persons were more knowledgeable, more aware, more dissatisfied with the existing notions about God. They were able to arrive at better notions of God because the questions they asked were more complicated and required better answers than the current notions about God provided. Through their efforts, people in general were moved forward and acquired a clearer notion of Who or What God is

or should be. These "philosophers" gradually thought of God as something different from people, something more than just a power or a force, something more than a superhuman being residing in a world of the gods. They began to think of God as having qualities or attributes that made God what He should be: complete, unlimited, unchanging, and eternal. They began to describe Him with such terms as Infinite, All-Powerful, and All-Good. They saw Him without limitations of any sort.

Because they thought of God as giving existence to all things, they thought of Him as having existence in Himself. That is, they thought of God as not dependent on anything else, as existing apart from and unrelated to any other existence. They described God as Absolutely Pure (without limitation), Absolutely Holy, Totally Supreme, Absolute Necessity, and Total Reality. In other words, they were able to say that God is not only what people can possibly conceive a God to be. He is beyond what people's limited minds can conceive. He is what is meant by the term "God."*

The second way that God revealed Himself at this time, and again gradually, was *historically*. He revealed Himself in the life experiences of a particular people, the Jews.

---

*We are describing here the development of the idea of God that took place in our culture—the development of the idea of God in the areas most influenced by Near Eastern, Greek, and Roman philosophy. At about the same time, more sophisticated ideas of God were developing in other areas of the world like China and India. What is common to all of these developments is that people were trying to find out Who and What God is. Their descriptions of God might differ, depending on their experience, but the effort was the same.

only as Lord of the Universe and the First Cause of everything that is, but as the Lord of history— people's Ultimate Ruler.

These two revelations prepared the way for the most startling revelation of all. Christians believe that God revealed Himself *in person,* in Jesus, who, they believe, is God expressing Himself humanly. Belief in Jesus as the Son of God who became a man is the heart of Christianity. It is what makes Christian belief different from the religious belief of all other religious people.

Read the following selections from the Old Testament and, in the space provided or on a separate sheet of paper, tell what each is about. Be prepared to show how it is part of how God revealed Himself historically.

Exodus 1:1–14

Exodus 19:1–8

Numbers 33 & 34

Psalm 20

You are already familiar with the story of how the Jewish people were formed into a religious people during their wanderings in the desert. You remember that they were led out of slavery in Egypt by Moses. You recall that they made a Covenant with God in the desert and finally settled in what is now Israel. You also know that this history is preserved in the Old Testament of the Bible.

The important thing to recall about this is that God gradually revealed Himself to these people in their experience of life. They experienced God as a saving God, as a God vitally and intimately interested in their affairs, as a God at once Unique, Concerned, and Personal. They experienced God not simply as Sole Creator, as distant, aloof, or "godlike." They experienced Him as a Dynamic Reality in their lives. They experienced Him not

Psalm 27 and 103

Psalm 44 and 109

What Jesus Reveals about Our God and Our Relationship with Him

The uniqueness of our God lies in the fact that we have experienced Him in person. For us, God is not only Creator, Lord of the Universe, and Lord of History. He is our Final Destiny. We know this about our God because of what we believe about Jesus.

In this brief survey of the development of the idea of God, we do not have time to discuss the life of Jesus completely. We can only dwell briefly on the one aspect of Jesus' life that led the Apostles to believe that Jesus was the expected Jewish Messiah and the Son of God. That was Jesus' resurrection from the dead.

We shall not dwell on proofs for the resurrection—that lies outside of our discussion for the moment. Neither shall we dwell on the nature of the act of resurrection. *Our concern is with its meaning.* If we accept (believe) the Apostles' experience of the risen Jesus, we accept also what this means.

Two important features of this meaning which affect our own religious faith are: (1) Jesus is alive now with a New Life we call his Risen Life, and (2) Jesus' resurrection gives us a clue to our final destiny. Both tell us something about our God. Properly understood, both can help us find a God we can believe in. This is the lesson of Jesus' life, death, and resurrection.

If we believe that Jesus is alive now, we believe that he lives and acts among his followers as he did during his visible, limited, earthly life, but in keeping with his new Risen Life. Just as Jesus lived and acted in his earthly life in himself and through his followers, so does he live and act today in himself and in his followers. He acts now in himself through the sacramental life of his body, the Church (see Colossians 1:18 and Ephesians 4:15–16), and through his followers by their influence on others. *Through the sacramental life of his Church and through his followers, Jesus is made visible to the world.*

This belief is at once a challenge and a joy for Christians who truly believe it. It is a challenge, for God, respecting people's freedom, leaves them to determine how effectively they will manifest Jesus to the world. Those of small belief and small motivation manifest Jesus only weakly (or even not at all). Those of great faith and strong motivation manifest Jesus strongly. This great mystery of God's way to manifest Himself to the world is a constant challenge to Christians generation after generation. It is also the answer to the ebb and flow of the influence of Christianity through the ages. God, as it were, leaves the revelation of Himself in Jesus up to the Christians of each age. The world is more or less conscious of God-in-Christ according to the response of Christians to their call to manifest God to the world.

Our Final Destiny

Jesus' resurrection gives us a clue to our final destiny and tells us more about our God. When God became a man in the person of Jesus, He entered His creation and bestowed on it His own Divine Life. *In Jesus, therefore, people were saved* from *a nondivine existence* for *a full share in the Divine Life.* They were to be caught up, as it were, and taken into the Divine Life completely and without reservation. But it is obvious that they could not be full sharers as long as they lived a limited, earthly life. Hence, they would have to experience a new life, a different dimension of existence beyond their experience of life as it now is. Jesus' resurrection leads us to believe that this new life will be ours after we pass through death (as he did) to the risen life he now shares with us in his Church and through his sacraments. **We believe that our unique sharing of the life of God begins in our sacramental association with God in our present life. It will come to its special fullness in our risen life, the life we now call our eternal life.**

What this tells us about our God is that He is at once transcendent (that is, beyond, above, and outside of ordinary human experience) and immanent (close to us, or dwelling within us). He is the cause of our existence, the sustainer of our life, and our absolute and final destiny. It also tells us that God has manifested Himself to us as a **triune God** (that is what we mean by "Trinity"). Because we experience God as **Creator** (Jesus called Him "Father"), as **Savior** (Jesus as Son of God saved creation from a nondivine existence), and as **Sanctifier** (God acts in the world directly and particularly through the Spirit of Jesus), we believe that God expresses Himself to us as three distinct Persons: Father, Son, and Spirit. In this way, Christians believe that God is not only Absolute and Essential Reality, complete and distinct from His creation, but is also present to and in His creation as its Principal Cause and its Saving Presence.

In the space below, or on a separate sheet of paper, give five things that Christians believe about their God.

No matter how much we think about God, many questions remain unanswered for us about God. On a separate sheet of paper or in the space provided below, write three or four questions about God and your belief in God that still need attention as far as you are concerned. When you have finished, catalogue your questions with the questions of your classmates and hold an open forum on the questions, seeking not confrontation but clarification.

1.2 Prayer as a Response to the Presence of God

Although it is true that most Christians do not understand all the philosophical and theological bases for their belief in the God of Christians, they do relate to Him "in the Christian way." They feel that they must keep in touch with God somehow, and the way they do it is through prayer. In other words, they pray as Christians pray.* Even so, most of them experience some difficulty with prayer from time to time—as most religious people do. It's natural.

As we said earlier, you experience highs and lows in your spiritual life just as you do in your physical, intellectual, and emotional life. Some days you feel good, other days you feel pretty blah. Some days you are pepped up, other days you don't care much at all. It's the same with prayer. Sometimes you feel like praying, other days you don't. Sometimes prayer comes easy, other times it's a chore. Some days you feel you "have to pray" (some mysterious inner feeling or need seems to direct you to pray, or you feel particularly helpless or inadequate and turn to prayer). Other days you don't feel any need at all. Once in a while prayer may seem to be the only answer. At other times even prayer may seem futile and hopeless. That's the way prayer-life is.

---

*People of other religious persuasions also keep in touch with their God in their own ways. Because this book discusses "Christian" worship, only Christian responses to the reality of God are discussed.

LAST NIGHT I PRAYED TO YOU FOR PATIENCE — — WHAT'S THE HOLDUP?

THAVES 7-21

Reprinted by permission. © 1981 NEA, Inc.

But over and above that, prayer may be difficult for some people because they have not kept up a prayer-life. For some reason or other they have more or less abandoned prayer, and they feel strange, embarrassed almost, to pray. Others, continuing their childhood habits, find prayer rather childish. It doesn't fit in with what they know of or experience in life as they grow up. For some others, experiencing particular difficulty, prayer has become a kind of routine, something they "do" every so often. It consists of a series of recited formulas that they don't think about very much, or, perhaps, don't understand or expect much from.

Other people experience difficulty with prayer because they expect too much.

They may expect, for example, to feel good every time they pray, or they expect something magical to happen—and it doesn't. Prayer, for them, is asking a favor from God (something they can't do themselves) and expecting immediate results, like saying a frantic prayer during a test and expecting God to give them the answer for something they didn't study for. For them, prayer is going to God in desperation.

There is nothing wrong, of course, with asking God for something, or with expecting results, or with feeling good when we pray. Praying for something is one aspect of prayer, and expecting results is natural. Neither one or both are the whole of prayer, however.

Prayer does not consist in battering the walls of heaven for personal benefits or the success of our plans. Rather it is the committing of ourselves for the carrying out of His purposes... It is not bending God's will to ours, but our will to God's.

Admitting, then, that prayer is sometimes difficult because we are human, and that some people have difficulty with prayer because they have false or inadequate notions of what prayer is, what can we do to make our prayer-life better?

Well, first of all, it seems that we ought to understand what prayer really is. In its broadest sense, prayer is a response to the presence of God. The response can be either personal or liturgical. If it is by an individual, it is personal prayer. If it is an official group response, it is liturgical prayer.

The reality of God's presence does not depend upon people's awareness of His presence or on their being able to experience His presence with their senses. God is present because He is God—whether a person realizes it or not. The important thing to remember (and this is where the discussion on Christian prayer begins) is that *Christian prayer is a positive response to our awareness of the presence of God*.

For example: Have you ever been riding in a car with a friend going, say, ten or fifteen miles per hour over the posted speed limit when you see a police car sitting on the side of the road with the radar antenna pointed in your direction? What's the reaction? Does your awareness of the presence of the police car make the policeman present?

So it is with the presence of God. Our awareness of God's presence and our relationship to Him determines our reaction. Our reaction, or response, is what constitutes our prayer-life. If we are truly aware, our prayer-life is strong and sure—we respond to God as He is known to us. If we are barely aware, or aware only of a duty to pray, our prayer-life

will be weak or "dutiful." Fortunately, God understands our limitations and our human inclinations, and accepts us as we are. He accepts our prayer-life as it now is. He offers us an opportunity to make it better (for example, by giving us this opportunity to reflect on it). He calls us to share His presence in a deep and lasting relationship.

Keeping in Touch with God

To develop such a relationship, we need to keep in touch with God through prayer. This is easy when we feel like praying, but what about praying when we don't feel like it? That's when we can determine what our prayer-life is really like.

It's not easy to pray when we're not in the mood, when we feel that it won't do any good, or when we feel that God doesn't listen. Everyone feels that way from time to time. So what should we do when it is difficult for us to pray? *We ought to pray whether we feel like it or not*. After all, if we never did anything unless we felt like it, we wouldn't do many things we know we ought to do, such as studying, or helping around the house, or going to the dentist. So it is with prayer. We ought to pray even when we don't feel like it because it is the human thing to do—it is the right thing. God is present, and we ought to respond to this presence.

The second thing we ought to do to keep in touch with God is *to develop a habit of prayer*. Developing a habit of prayer is like developing any other habit: the more often we do it correctly, the easier it becomes. (St. John Baptist de la Salle used to tell his followers and the boys

> # LONELINESS IS BEING UNAWARE OF ONE THAT IS WITH US EVERYWHERE.
>
> — EDWARD A. GLOEGGLER

and girls he taught to recall God's presence by saying to themselves: "Let us remember that we are in the holy presence of God.") By actually saying a short prayer before you begin something, you will develop a habit of praying that becomes almost second nature to you. If you get into the habit of praying at specific times every day, as many people do, for example, on rising in the morning or on retiring, or before and after meals, or after school, or during periods of stress or difficulty, your habit of prayer will become almost a reflex action.

The third thing we ought to do to develop a good prayer-life is *to try to pray better*. We should not let our prayers become routine. We should meditate often on Who and What God is for us. Even when we do not feel like praying, to try to pray better will affect our mood, and our attention will be drawn away from ourselves to God, and our prayer will be better.

Through such prayer practices we keep in touch with God, and our relationship with him becomes more mature—in keeping with our maturing selves.

If you are interested in improving your prayer life, it is important to reflect on its present condition and to work at improving it. Take a minute or two to think about your prayer life as it is now using the questions below as starters. After each question write in the appropriate word that reflects how your prayer life is now.

Is your general prayer life alive and well or is it weak and barely surviving?

Is it in keeping with your physical, intellectual, and emotional growth or is it about like it was four or five years ago?

Is it a response to what you know and feel about God or is it just going through the motions most of the time or just reciting formulas?

Do you pay attention to prayer only during periods of great need or when you are distressed?

Does your prayer life reflect a true relationship with the God you believe in?

Are you satisfied with your prayer life as it is?

If you are unhappy with your prayer-life, it's not strange. You are experiencing the normal ups and downs of your spiritual life, and it's an indication that you are not satisfied with what passes for prayer for you. It means that you are looking for an adult prayer-life, and that you are ready to think more deeply about this strange mystery of human existence: your relationship with God. It means that you are growing up spiritually.

Christian Prayer Is a Response to the Saving Presence of God

As you know, Christians believe that God created people to share His Divine Life with them. They believe that this sharing entered its final stage when Jesus, the Son of God, became a human being. By so doing, Catholics believe, Jesus filled all of creation with his Divine Life and saved creation from a nondivine existence. Catholics further believe that because Jesus is alive and acting in and through the Church, they are being saved by this saving presence in the

Church. This saving presence, for Catholics, however is not an abstract principle, a pious thought, or simply a general saving presence. For them it is real. It is personal, sacramental, and social. It is to this presence that Catholics respond in prayer.

It is **personal** in two ways. First, it is experienced in the person of Christ who is present and alive in his Church. As Jesus said:

> When I go, you will not be left all alone; I will come back to you. In a little while the world will see me no more, but you will see me; and because I live, you also will live. When that day comes, you will know that I am in my Father and that you are in me, just as I am in you. (John 14:18–20)

Second, it is experienced in the personal lives of each Christian because God lives with them and in them, filling them with His life. Jesus, responding to a question, said:

> "Whoever loves me will obey my teaching. My Father will love him, and my Father and I will come to him and live with him. I will ask the Father, and he will give you another Helper, who will stay with you forever. He is the Spirit, who reveals the truth about God. The world cannot receive him, because it cannot see him or know him. But you know him, because he remains with you and is in you." (John 14:23,16,17)

God's saving presence is **sacramental** because God acts in the lives of Christians in a specific, purposeful, and immediate way in the sacraments of the Church. They are signs of Christ acting in a specific, purposeful, and immediate way in his Church. This we know from the Gospels:

When the people found Jesus on the other side of the lake they said to him, "Teacher, when did you get here?"

Jesus answered: "I tell you the truth: you are looking for me because you ate the bread and had all you wanted, not because you saw my works of power. Do not work for food that spoils; instead, work for the food that lasts for eternal life. This food the Son of Man will give you, because God, the Father, has put his mark of approval on him." They asked him then, "What can we do in order to do God's works?" Jesus answered, "This is the work God wants you to do: believe in the one he sent." They replied: "What sign of power will you perform so that we may see it and believe you? What will you do? Our ancestors ate manna in the desert, just as the scripture says: 'He gave them bread from heaven to eat.'" "I tell you the truth," Jesus said. "What Moses gave you was not the bread from heaven; it is my Father who gives you the real bread from heaven. For the bread that God gives is he who comes down from heaven and gives life to the world." "Sir," they asked him, "give us this bread always." "I am the bread of life," Jesus told them. "He who comes to me will never be hungry; he who believes in me will never be thirsty. . . .

"I tell you the truth: he who believes has eternal life.

"I am the bread of life. Your ancestors ate the manna in the desert, but died. But the bread which comes down from heaven is such that whoever eats it will not die. I am the living bread which came down from heaven. If anyone eats this bread he will live for ever. And the bread which I will give him is my flesh, which I give so that the world may live."

This started an angry argument among the Jews. "How can this man give us his flesh to eat?" they asked.

Jesus said to them: "I tell you the truth if you do not eat the flesh of the Son of Man and drink his blood you will not have life in yourselves. Whoever eats my flesh and drinks my blood has eternal life, and I will raise him to life on the last day. For my flesh is the real food, my blood is the real drink. Whoever eats my flesh and drinks my blood lives in me and I live in him. The living Father sent me, and because of him I live also. In the same way, whoever eats me will live because of me.

"This, then, is the bread that came down from heaven; it is not like the bread that your ancestors ate and then died. The one who eats this bread will live for ever." (John 6:25–35;47–58)

God's saving presence is **social** because He expresses His presence through the members of His Church which is His body. It is through them that Jesus expresses who and what he is for the world. Just as you express who and what you are through your body, so does Jesus express himself through the Church. As St. Paul said in his letters:

It was in one Spirit that all of us . . . were baptized into one body. . . . You, then, are the body of Christ. Every one of you is a member of it. (1 Corinthians 12:13,27) Continually we carry about in our bodies the dying of Jesus, so that in our bodies the life of Jesus may also be revealed.

While we live we are constantly being delivered to death for Jesus' sake, so that the life of Jesus may be revealed in our mortal flesh. (2 Corinthians 4:10,11)

For Catholics, then, God's presence is not just "there" like an outsider at a party. It is a real presence, a presence that is necessary to the group. For Catholics, God's presence is as God's presence should be: close, reliable, effective, and saving. It should move them from their limited existence in their earthly lives to the full experience of Him in eternity. **It is to this presence that Catholics respond in prayer.**

Jesus Tells Us Who God Is for Us

The best example, of course, of response to God's loving, saving presence in the world is Jesus' own prayer. He gave it to his Apostles when they asked him to teach them how to pray. He not only showed them how to pray, but also how to think of their relationship with God. In telling of this incident, St. Luke says:

> Jesus said to them, "When you pray, say this:
> 'Father:
> May your holy name be honored; may your Kingdom come.
> Give us day by day the food we need.
> Forgive us our sins,
>   for we forgive everyone who does us wrong.
> And do not bring us to hard testing.' " (Luke 11:2–4)*

What Jesus is saying, of course, is that when we pray, we should think of God as our Father, not as some harsh ruler or imposing Lord forcing His will on His subjects. He wants us to think of God as caring, concerned, and interested in each of us just as a good father is interested in and cares for each of his children. He is telling us that we should not think of God as far away, unreachable, and indifferent, waiting for adoration and submission. We should, rather, think of God as One who wants us to come to Him, to trust Him, realizing that He is willing to hear us and anxious to help us. It is to this God that Jesus wants us to respond in prayer.

*The more common form of "The Lord's Prayer" is found in Matthew 6:9–13.

Take a few moments to compare your present idea of and feelings toward God with the image of God given by Jesus. When you have done this, on a separate sheet of paper, write a brief composition about how a Christian should think of God and how one should respond to this God.

Compose a prayer which reflects what you have written above.

From your own experience tell what you think most people think of God. In the space below or on a separate sheet of paper summarize what you think is the idea of God of the average adult. When you have done this, do the same for your classmates or your neighborhood friends.

On the next several pages are examples of how some people have responded to the presence of God in their lives. We have called these pages "A Book of Prayers." The prayers of some Christians are given with Group I. A few samples of non-Christian prayer are given in Group II.

Some people, interested in improving their prayer life, have found that looking at, thinking about, and praying with the prayers of others is helpful. That is why "A Book of Prayers" is given in your book. Look at these prayers, and think about them. Let them teach you to pray.

A Book of Prayers

To Love: The Prayer of Adolescent

I want to love, Lord, I need to love.
All my being is desire; My heart, My
    body, yearn in the night towards an
    unknown one to love.
My arms thrash about, and I can seize on
    no object for my love.
I am alone and want to be two.
I speak, and no one is there to listen.
I live, and no one is there to share my life.
Why be so rich and have no one to enrich?
Where does this love come from?
Where is it going?
I want to love, Lord, I need to love.
Here this evening, Lord, is all my love,
    unused.

Listen, son, Stop, and make, silently, a
    long pilgrimage to the bottom of your
    heart.
Walk by the side of your love so new, as
    one follows a brook to find its source,

And at the very end, deep within you, in
    the infinite mystery of your troubled
    soul, you will meet me.
For I call myself Love, son.
And from the beginning I have been
    nothing but Love, And Love is in you.

It is I who made you to love, To love
    eternally;
And your love will pass through another
    self of yours—
It is she that you seek; Set your mind at
    rest; she is on your way,
    on the way since the beginning,
    the way of my love.
You must wait for her coming.
She is approaching, You are approaching.
You will recognize each other,
For I've made her body for you,
I've made yours for her.
I've made your heart for her,
I've made hers for you,
And you seek each other, in the night.
In "my night," which will become Light
    if you trust me.

Keep yourself for her, son,
As she is keeping herself for you.
I shall keep you for one another,
And, since you hunger for love, I've put on
    your way all your brothers to love.
Believe me, it's a long apprenticeship,
    learning to love,
And there are not several kinds of love:
Loving is always leaving oneself to go
    towards others. . . .

Lord, help me to forget myself for others,
    my brothers,
That in giving myself I may teach myself
    to love.

—**Michael Quoist**

A Parent's Prayer

O heavenly Father, make me a better parent. Teach me to understand my children, to listen patiently to what they have to say, and to answer all their questions kindly. Keep me from interrupting them or contradicting them. Make me as courteous to them as I would have them be to me.

Forbid that I should ever laugh at their mistakes, or resort to shame or ridicule when they displease me. May I never punch them for my own selfish satisfaction or to show my power.

Let me not tempt my child to lie or steal. And guide me hour by hour that I may demonstrate by all I say and do that honesty produces happiness.

Reduce, I pray, the meanness in me. And when I am out of sorts, help me, O Lord, to hold my tongue.

May I ever be mindful that my children are children and I should not expect of them the judgment of adults.

Let me not rob them of the opportunity to wait on themselves and to make decisions.

Bless me with the bigness to grant them all their reasonable requests, and the courage to deny them privileges I know will do them harm.

Make me fair and just and kind. And fit me, O Lord, to be loved and respected and imitated by my children. Amen.

A Prayer for Americans

Lord, I thank thee . . .
For the healing beauty of flowers—
welcome balm for the battered spirit . . .
For the exciting wonder of new life as
    manifested in the smallest
    creatures . . .
For the majesty of trees that protect our
    soil, husband our waters, provide us
    shelter . . .
For the mysterious process of plant growth
    and endless bounty of fields that
    nourish my body.

Help me to understand that life on earth
    is part of an awe-inspiring pattern,
    with man the chief steward.
Teach me to appreciate the delicate
    relationship of all things on earth:
The majesty of an elk . . .
The spring time promise of a pussy
    willow . . .
The crystal purity of a dew drop.

Lord, teach me my proper place
Guide me in doing my part to solve the
    problems that beset us.
Let me be as dedicated to this task as a
    bee gathering pollen.
Show me how to draw inspiration from the

daily miracles I can witness on any
    walk in the outdoors.
Help me remember that a song and a
    smile are more in tune with life than a
    wail or a groan.
Make me realize that just as in nature
    there is both tranquility and power—
    so that capacity also resides in me.

Please give me humility to see how crude
    the most spectacular man-made thing is
    compared with . . .
A baby rabbit . . .
The wondrous perfection of a
    snowflake . . .
Or the grandeur of a 4,000-year-old
    bristlecone pine.
Give me the wisdom to know that if our
    environment fails wildlife then I, too,
    am doomed.

Lord, open my eyes . . .
Help me to understand that we are indeed
    all God's Creatures.
This is my prayer—
I hope a prayer for all Americans.
Amen.

—Bob Strohm

Reprinted from the December–January 1972 issue of
National Wildlife Magazine, copyright 1972 by the
National Wildlife Federation.

Prayer for the United States

*Lord, I speak to You with
gratitude.
On every side I see the
abundant blessings You
have given to our country.
Even when we face sorrow and
sufferings, our burdens are
light compared to our
brothers and sisters in the
human family.*

*Increase in us, Lord, the gift
of faith so that we might
see all men as Your sons.
Don't let us be blind to our
brotherhood in Christ
because of the different
color of our skin.
Don't let us be deaf to Your
command of love because
of our different political
systems.
Don't let us become isolated
in fear of one another
because of race or creed or
difference of age.*

*Help us whom You have
blessed so abundantly to
reach out and touch with
generosity the lives of the
poor.
Give us the grace to share the
goods of our creation.
Give us the courage to help
our mighty nation to use its
power to bring freedom and
dignity to all peoples.*

*Help each of us—whoever and
wherever we are—to realize
that our lives may be the
only copy of the Gospels
that our neighbor may ever
read.
Amen.*

For Brotherhood through Prayer

*O Lord, our heavenly Father,
You hear us praying.
You hear our brothers praying
in Africa, in Asia, in
Australia, in America, in
Europe, in Latin America.*

*We are all one in prayer.
We praise and honor You
and we beg You that we may
rightly carry out Your
commission
to witness and to love
in our church and
throughout the whole
world.*

*We ask you to accept our
prayers graciously
even when they might sound
strange or confused.
We ask for our own needs
and those of our brothers
and depend on Your under-
standing to guide us
and open our hearts to unity
in Jesus Christ our Lord.
Amen.*

Prayer from Apollo 8

*Give us, O God the vision which can see
Thy love in the world in spite of human
failure.*

*Give us the faith, the trust, the goodness in
spite of our ignorance and weakness.*

*Give us the knowledge that we may
continue to pray with understanding
hearts and show us what each one of us
can do to set forth the coming of the
day of universal peace.*

A Prayer for the Dead

Let us pray—
Whenever we face death,
Father, it is always new, fresh
    and painful.
It means mystery and fear for
    us, as well as separation.
Yet in your Son you have
    made us one.
His promise of risen life
    where we will at last be
    free sustains us and gives
    us hope.

We pray, then, for our brother
    (sister) N.,
for all the dying and for
    ourselves,

that the life we know so well
    may be pale
beside the life that we shall
    see.
We ask this through Christ
    our Lord.

O Lord it is easy to dwell with
    You!
So easy for me to believe in
    You!
When Spirit clouds over and
    I, crushed, am made dumb
When even the smartest
    people know not what
    tomorrow will bring
You bestow the clear
    assuredness of being
Vigilantly keeping the

channels of Goodness
    unclogged.
Surpassing thus the summit
    of earthly glory
I behold the Way, which alone
    I never could have found
Wondrous Way, opposite to
    despair,

Whence myself shall become
    the reflection of Your
    world.
What need have I to speak
    what You alone shall
    reveal to me, and if I find
    not the time to carry it
    through
It means You've chosen others
    for the task.
                    —Alexander Solzhenitzen

Prayer for Missioners

*Father of all, Lord of
  creation!
Please guide and bless the
  missioners—
priests and sisters, brothers
  and doctors,
nurses and teachers—all who
  are willing
to dedicate their lives to
  others in Your service.
Bless their work throughout
  the world.
Pour out Your Holy Spirit
  upon them.
Strengthen them in weakness.
Comfort them in trials.
Be at their side in all their
  labors and joys.*

*Open the minds and
  hearts of men to
the message of love in
  Your Gospel
preached and lived by Your
  missioners
and witnessed by the joy of
  their lives.
Grant them a soaring spirit of
  love,
health of body and mind
that they may by their life
and work,
discover the true message of
  peace, love and
justice with those among
whom they live.*

*May their lives give witness to
  the brotherhood
which will make Your name
  known
and loved by all men through
  Christ our Lord.
Amen.*

Psalm 23
(Translated for American
Indians by an unknown missioner)

*The Great Father Above is a
  shepherd chief;
I am His and I want not.
He holds out to me a rope,
  and the name of that rope is
  Love.
And He draws me and he
  draws me
To a place where the grass is
  green and the water is not
  dangerous.
Sometimes my heart is heavy
  and I fall down,
But he lifts me up and
  comforts me.*

*Sometimes He makes the rope
  into a whip,
But afterwards He gives me
  his staff to lean on!
He lays His hand on my head
  and all the "tired" is gone.
His name is Wonderful!
Sometime—it may be soon, it
  may be a long, long time—
He will lead me into a place
  between the mountains;
It is dark there, but I will not
  be afraid
I will not draw back.*

*For it is in there between the
  mountains
That the Shepherd Chief will
  meet me,
And the hunger I have felt
  along the way
Will be satisfied,
And I will dwell in His House
  forever.*

Prayer for Vocations to Mission

*God, grant to Your Christian people
everywhere the grace to make the
Gospel live in their lives
That they may speak its message to all
men, not with their lips alone but with
deeds which declare their faith loud and
clear, like a hymn sung by a thousand
voices.
Give us God, the courage to commit
ourselves to You and through You to
every man:*

*For how can we pretend to love you whom
we do not see, unless we love our
neighbor, whom we do see.
Let us discover You in the peoples and
customs and cultures of other lands.
Give us young men and women from our
homes, our communities, our nation
who will dedicate their lives to bring
Your love to our brothers as Your
missioners.
For Your Son came to cast fire on the
earth and He wishes it to be kindled.*

An Indian Prayer

O' Great Spirit,
Whose voice I hear in the winds,
And whose breath gives life to all the
    world, hear me! I am small and weak,
I need your strength and wisdom.

Let me walk in beauty, and make my eyes
    ever behold the red and purple sunset.
Make my hands respect the things you
    have made and my ears sharp to hear
    your voice.

Make me wise so that I may understand
    things you have taught my people.
Let me learn the lessons you have hidden
    in every leaf and rock.
I seek strength, not to be greater than my
    brother, but to fight my greatest
    enemy—myself.
Make me always ready to come to you
    with clean hands and straight eyes.

So when life fades, as the fading sunset,
    my spirit may come to you without
    shame.

An Indian Christmas Carol

'Twas in the moon of winter-time
When all the birds had fled,
That mighty Gitchee Manitou
Sent angel choirs instead.
Before their light the stars grew dim,
And wandering hunters heard the hymn:

Jesus your king is born, Jesus is born!
In excelsis gloria!

Within a lodge of broken bark,
A tender Babe was found.
A ragged robe of rabbit-skin
Had wrapped His beauty round.
The chiefs from far before Him knelt,
With gifts of fox and beaver pelts.

O children of the forest free,
O sons of Manitou,
The holy Child of earth and heav'n
Is born today for you.
Come kneel before the radiant Boy
Who brings you beauty, peace, and joy.

A Community Prayer to the Holy Spirit

Leader: Come, Holy Spirit, fill the hearts
    of your faithful.
All: And kindle in them the fire of
    your love.
Leader: Lord, send out your Spirit.

All: And renew the face of the earth.

Leader: Let us pray—
    Father, you taught the hearts of
    your faithful people by sending
    them the light of your Holy
    Spirit. In that Spirit give us right
    judgment and the joy of his
    comfort and guidance. We ask this
    through Christ our Lord.
All: Amen.

*Glory be to the Father and to the Son, and
the Holy Spirit, as it was in the beginning
is now, and shall be forever.*

*Hail, Mary, full of grace, the Lord is with
you. Blessed are you among women, and
blessed is the fruit of your womb, Jesus.
Holy Mary, Mother of God, pray for us
sinners now, and at the hour of our death.*
            **—Devotional prayer from
            the Sixteenth Century**

*Bless us, O Lord, and these Your gifts
which we are about to receive from Your
goodness through Christ our Lord.*
            —Standard blessing before meals

Lord, Teach Us to Pray

My Father in heaven,
I give reverence to You.
I want Your kingdom among
    people to come to be
So that Your plan for people
    will be realized.
Help me to secure the needs
    of my body.
Forgive me my not truly
    human choices
While I learn to forgive those
Who treat me shabbily.
Let me not become a victim
Of my weakness, selfishness
    and egotism.
Give me the strength to do
    what is right.

Lord, make me an instrument
    of your peace.
Where there is hatred, let me
    sow love;
where there is injury, pardon;
where there is doubt, faith
where there is despair, hope;
where there is darkness, light;
where there is sadness, joy.

O Divine Master, grant that I
    may not seek
to be consoled as to console;
to be understood, as to under-
    stand;
to be loved, as to love.
For it is in giving that we
    receive;
it is in pardoning that we are
    pardoned;
and it is in dying that we are
    born to eternal life.
                    —St. Francis of Assisi

The Church's Prayer of Praise

Glory to God in the highest,
    and peace to his people on
    earth.
Lord God, heavenly King,
    almighty God and Father,
we worship you,
we give you thanks,
we praise you for your glory.

Lord Jesus Christ, only Son
    of the Father,
Lord God, Lamb of God,
you take away the sin of the
    world:
have mercy on us;
you are seated at the right
hand of the Father:
receive our prayer.

For you alone are the Holy
    One,
you alone are the Lord,
you alone are the Most High,
    Jesus Christ, with the
    Holy Spirit, in the glory
    of God the Father.
Amen.

The Prayer of Mary

My soul proclaims the
greatness of the Lord,
my spirit rejoices in God my
Savior
for he has looked with favor
on his lowly servant.
From this day all generations
will call me blessed:
the Almighty has done great
things for me,
and holy is his Name.
He has mercy on those who
fear him in every
generation.
He has shown the strength of
his arm,
he has scattered the proud in
their conceit.
He has cast down the mighty
from their thrones,
and has lifted up the lowly.
He has filled the hungry with
good things,
and the rich he has sent away
empty.
He has come to the help of
his servant Israel
for he has remembered his
promise of mercy,
the promise he made to our
fathers,
to Abraham and his children
forever.

—**Luke 1:46–55**

Grace at Mealtime

Thank you for this food, Lord, thank you. We're grateful that we can eat when we're hungry. We're also happy and grateful that we can do it together and not be alone, with each other or you.

Nourish our bodies and minds as well as our souls. Make us stronger, especially in our wills, so that we can serve you and others instead of just asking favors for ourselves. Show us the real needs of others, Jesus. You told us that when we do anything to any of your brothers—and ours—in the world, we actually do it to you. When, Lord, do we pass you by because we pass by one of our brothers who is in need? Teach us to see your face, Jesus, when we look into our brothers' faces.

Thank you for this knowledge of you and our brothers. Thank you for energy and strength, mercy and love. Amen.

From *Are You Running with Me, Jesus?* by Malcolm Boyd. Copyright © 1965 by Malcolm Boyd. Reprinted by permission of Holt, Rinehart and Winston, Publishers.

Morning Prayer

When little things would irk me, and I grow
Impatient with my dear ones, make me know
How in a moment joy can take its flight
And happiness be quenched in endless night.
Keep this thought with me all the livelong day
That I may guard the harsh words I might say
When I would fret and grumble, fiery hot,
At trifles that tomorrow are forgot—
Let me remember, Lord, how it would be
If these, my loved ones, were not here with me.

Cardinal Newman's Prayer

O Lord, support us all the day long of this
troublous life, until the shadows lengthen, and
the evening comes, and the busy world is
hushed, and the fever of life is over, and our
work is done.

Then of thy great mercy grant us a safe lodging,
and a holy rest, and peace at last.
Through Jesus Christ our Lord.
Amen.

—John Henry Newman

Let Me Give

I do not know how long I'll live
But while I live, Lord, let me give
Some comfort to someone in need
By smile or nod—kind word or deed
And let me do what e'er I can
To ease things for my fellow man.
I want naught but to do my part
To "lift" a tired or weary heart,
To change folks frowns to smiles again—
Then I will not have lived in vain
And I'll not care how long I'll live
If I can give—and give—and give.

—Joe Hoviss

Let My Life Sing

Make me too brave to lie or be unkind,
Make me too understanding, too, to mind
The little hurts companions give, and
*   friends,*
The careless hurts that no one quite
*   intends.*
May I forget
What ought to be forgotten, and recall,
Unfailing, all

That ought to be recalled, each kindly
*   thing.*
Forgetting what might sting
To all upon my way,
Day after day,
Let me be joy, be hope! Let my life sing!

—Mary Carolyn Davies

From *Lines to Live By* © 1972 by Clinton T. Howell,
published by Thomas Nelson, Inc., reprinted by
permission of Peggy H. Howell

Psalm 148

(From the Hebrew Bible: perhaps composed around 1,000 B.C.)

Praise the LORD!

Praise the LORD from heaven, you that live in the heights above.
Praise him, all his angels, all his heavenly armies.

Praise him, sun and moon; praise him, shining stars.
Praise him, highest heavens and the waters above the sky.

Let them all praise the name of the LORD!
He commanded, and they were created; by his command they were fixed in their places forever, and they cannot disobey.

Praise the LORD from the earth, sea monsters and all ocean depths; lightning and hail, snow and clouds strong winds that obey his command.

Praise him, hills and mountains, fruit trees and forests; all animals, tame and wild, reptiles and birds.

Praise him, kings and all peoples, princes and all other rulers; girls and young men, old people and children too.
Let them all praise the name of the LORD!
His name is greater than all others; his glory is above earth and heaven.
He made his nation strong, so that all his people praise him—the people of Israel, so dear to him.

Praise the LORD!

A Moslem Prayer
(Adapted from the practices of Mohammad: 600 A.D.)

Thanks be to my Lord; He the Adorable, and only to be adored. My Lord, the Eternal, the Ever-existing, the Cherisher, the True Sovereign whose mercy and might overshadow the universe; the Regulator of the world, and Light of the creation. His is our worship; to Him belongs all worship;

He existed before all things, and will exist after all that is living has ceased. Thou art the adored, my Lord; Thou art the Master, the Loving and Forgiving. . . . O my Lord, Thou art the Helper of the afflicted, the Reliever of all distress, the Consoler of the broken-hearted; Thou art present everywhere to help Thy servants . . .

O my Lord, Thou art the Creator, I am only created; Thou art my Sovereign, I am only Thy servant; Thou art the Helper, I am the beseecher; Thou art the Forgiver, I am the sinner; Thou, my Lord, art the Merciful, All-knowing, All-loving.

Quoted in *The Religions of Man*, Huston Smith, Perennial Library (New York: Harper & Row, 1958), p. 239.

To Aton
(Egyptian God: 1360 B.C.*)

How manifold it is, what thou hast made!
They are hidden from the face of man.
O sole god, like whom there is no other!

Thou didst create the world according to thy desire,
Whilst thou wert alone:
All men, cattle, and wild beasts,
Whatever is on earth, going upon its feet,
And what is on high, flying with its wings.

The countries of Syria and Nubia, the land of Egypt,
Thou settest every man in his place,
Thou suppliest their necessities. . . .

From "Egyptian Hymns and Prayers," transl. John A. Wilson in James B. Pritchard, *Ancient Near Eastern Texts Relating to the Old Testament*, 3rd. rev. edn., with Supplement (copyright 1969 by Princeton University Press), p. 370. Reprinted by permission of Princeton University Press.

*There are, at present, no records of formal prayers from civilizations we now call prehistoric (pre-historic meaning before the age of writing). As archaeologists continue their research into ancient ruins, they are discovering more and more artifacts associated with prehistoric people. Among these artifacts are evidences of solemn ceremonies and elaborate rituals directed to the gods of pre-historic people. No doubt there were chants and invocations addressed to the gods accompanying these rituals and ceremonies.

Hymn to Zeus
(Greek Supergod: 1000 B.C.)

O God most glorious, called by many a
name,
Nature's great King, through endless years
the same;
Omnipotence, who by thy just decree
Controllest all, hail Zeus, for unto thee
Behoves thy creatures in all lands to call

From *The Stoic and Epicurean Philosophers,* W. J.
Oates (New York: Random House, 1940).

A Hindu Invocation

O Lord, forgive three sins that are due to
my human limitations:
Thou art everywhere, but I worship you
here;
Thou art without form, but I worship you
in these forms;
Thou needest no praise, yet I offer you
these prayers and salutations.
Lord, forgive three sins that are due to my
human limitations.

Quoted in *The Religions of Man,* Huston Smith,
Perennial Library (New York: Harper & Row, 1958),
p. 42.

I Had a Dream

I dreamed I was walking along the beach with the Lord. Across the sky flashed scenes from my life. I noticed two sets of footprints in the sand; one belonged to me, the other to the Lord. After the last scene of my life flashed before us, I looked back at the footprints in the sand. I noticed that many times along the path of my life, there was only one set of footprints. I also realized that it happened at the very lowest and saddest times in my life. I questioned the Lord about it.

"Lord, You said that once I decided to follow You, You would walk with me all the way. But I have noticed that during the most troublesome times in my life, there is only one set of footprints. I don't understand why in times when I needed You most, You would leave."

The Lord replied, "My precious one, I would never leave you during your times of trial and suffering. When you see only one set of footprints, it was then that I carried you."

1.4 Keeping in Touch with God in a Special Way

As we said on page 32, St. Paul tells us that we are all part of the body of Christ. He emphasizes the fact that "all the members, many though they are, are one body." He then goes on to say:

In the church God has put all in place: in the first place apostles, in the second place prophets, and in the third place teachers; then those who perform miracles, followed by those who are given the power to heal or to help others or to direct them or to speak in strange tongues. They are not all apostles or prophets or teachers. Not everyone has the power to work miracles or to heal diseases or to speak in strange tongues or to explain what is said.
(1 Corinthians 12:28–30)

What St. Paul is saying is that God has called each Christian to express his Christianity in a way that is special to him or her. He has established special and particular ways of life and ministry within Christianity for the good of the body of Christ itself and for its mission. Among these are the men and women you are undoubtedly familiar with: the religious sisters, brothers, and priests. You have experienced them—or at least seen them—in the Catholic schools, hospitals, day care centers, and any place where their special ministry is needed.

Who Are These Sisters, Brothers, and Priests?

From the very beginning of Christianity, some Christian men and women have been called by God to express their Christianity in the specific way we now call "the religious life." We do not have time now to discuss the history of the development of "the religious life" as we now know it, but the mode of expressing the Christian life known as "the religious

life" is a reality that needs to be examined and considered by all Christians.

Putting it simply, the religious life is an expression of Christianity which puts its primary emphasis on prayer and activities appropriate to religion.* Activities engaged in by people in religious life, such as teaching, nursing, caring for orphans or the poor, missionary activity, writing, publishing, making vestments, and so forth, are part of the life of a religious. They flow from or are expressions of their religious life.

This does not mean to say that Christians who are not "religious" are not religious. What it means is that those who are "religious" devote their lives primarily to prayer and religious pursuits. They set aside, as far as possible, activities which are not "religious" and spend their time principally on private, public, and liturgical prayer, and on things associated with their religious life.

Christians believe that being a Christian is a response to God's call to believe in Christ. Because all Christians are called by God to pursue their Christianity in a way that is special to them, we speak of Christianity as a "vocation"—a call by God to be Christ to the world. Some Christians, as we have said, have a special call to be "religious." This call, or vocation, is also selective. It is not given to every Christian. It is also indiscriminate. It knows no class, nor sex, nor status. People "in religion" are of all shapes and sizes, all intellectual levels, all abilities and capabilities, all temperaments and inclinations, all strengths and weaknesses. What they have in common is a dedication to a way of life that has God and His affairs as its principle endeavor.

Although anyone who is thus dedicated is "religious," "a religious," as we now use the term, is a man or a woman who is an accepted member of a group or community recognized by the Church as a religious order, congregation, or institute. Every such person vows or promises to live according to a religious rule or way of life of a community approved by the Pope or a bishop and pursues an activity in keeping with the purpose of the group to which he or she belongs.*

---

*Other religions have "religious" also. There are, for example, Buddhist monks, and many ancient religions, such as the Egyptian, Greek, Roman, and Incan, had their "vestal virgins." Although we are considering in this book only the Catholic Christian expression of the religious life, it is important to know that other Christian persuasions, such as the Lutherans, Anglicans, and Presbyterians, have "religious" also.

---

*A woman religious is most often called "Sister." In some cases women religious are called "Nuns." A male religious who is not ordained for the Eucharistic celebration is called a "Brother." A priest may or may not be a member of a religious order. If he is, he usually identifies himself by the name of the group or by its official initials, like SVD, OCSO, O Carm, and so forth.

What Do Religious Do?

There are many religious orders or institutes in the Catholic Church. Each has its own purpose, mode of expressing its prayer life, basic philosophy, and "secular" activity. In general, religious orders or institutes can be divided into two broad categories: contemplative and mission. Contemplative religious are those who devote themselves principally to the objective worship of God—through public recitation of the Divine Office and the solemn community Mass—and to contemplation.* They exclude external work

*To contemplate means to think seriously, consider thoroughly, or give continued attention to something. In religious life it means reflecting seriously and often on God and the things of God.

and all other things that would interfere with their public prayer, their community Mass, and their contemplative life. Among the more commonly known contemplative orders are the Carthusian, the Camaldolese, and Cistercian monks, and the Carthusian, Carmelite, and Poor Clare nuns. Certain branches of the Benedictine Order, both for men and for women, are contemplative, but most are also involved in mission activities.

The mission orders or institutes in the Catholic Church are those whose daily pursuits are the works of charity, such as teaching, nursing, preaching, giving retreats, caring for orphans, and so forth. The private and public prayer-life of religious engaged in mission activities, though important and the source of their

spiritual energy, is engaged in in places and at times outside of their works of charity.

Among the more commonly known mission orders and institutes in the United States and Canada are the Franciscans, Dominicans, Augustinians, Jesuits, Carmelites, Maryknoll Fathers and Sisters, Christian Brothers, Alexian Brothers, Daughters of Charity, Ursulines, Little Sisters of the Poor, Little Brothers of the Poor, and the Sisters of Loretto. By far the greater number of religious men and women are in mission orders or congregations. In the United States and Canada there are over 600 different groups of religious: nearly 500 groups of nuns, 125 groups of religious priests, and 30 groups of brothers.

Religious life, in any form, is a sign established by God to remind people that they are called to holiness, and that prayer and the works of charity are, or ought to be, the hallmarks of Christianity.

1.5 Who Are the Saints?

If any persons can be said to have kept in touch with God in a special way, it has been the saints.

While it is true that all Christians are saints because of the special grace that God has given them,* the term *saint* is

*From the very first days of the Christian communities, Christians were called "holy ones" or "saints" because they had received God's special grace in Christ which had transformed them. In his Epistle to the Ephesians (2:11–19), St. Paul says: "You are strangers and aliens no longer. No, you are fellow citizens of the saints. . . ."

given to those particular Christians who have been declared saints by the Church through its official process of beatification and canonization.

The Church does not canonize all saintly people, of course—their number is too great, and known only to God. Moreover it does not canonize certain people simply because they are good, or because they did some strange or wonderful thing. It does not canonize them, either, simply to honor them for the holiness of their lives. *The Church canonizes people for the community. It calls attention to the action of God in the life of the person, and reminds all Christians of their own call to holiness.*

The variety of saints attests to that fact. The list of saints includes people who were rich and poor, healthy and sick, bright and not-so-bright, young, middle-aged, and old, men and women, people of extraordinary energy and persons who led quiet, secluded lives. It includes popes, bishops, priests, religious, lay people, rulers and those governed, free men and slaves. It includes people from every walk of life and every temperament, and people from every historical age and every country.

Even though the saints came from various backgrounds and from every historical period and country, and even though their holiness manifested itself in a variety of ways, they all had one thing in common: a firm commitment of the things of God. They all had a strong sense of purpose and pursued their commitment with fidelity, dedicating themselves to God and His works above all else. They were very aware of the reality of God in their lives. It dominated their lives and impelled them to do what they did. It caused them to put all other things

> # A saint is one who makes goodness attractive.
>
> ### Laurence Housman

aside in favor of their pursuit. It was this that made them holy, made them saints. They were saints because they kept in intimate touch with God.

To appreciate the saints, and sanctity, you must remember that the saints were not born saints. They grew in holiness. They lived in the same world and in similar circumstances as the people among whom they lived. They shared the same limitations, the same hardships, the same temptations, the same challenges, the same opportunities, the same sacraments, and the same means to holiness that all Christians do. The only difference between the saints and other Christians is that from the moment of their dedication (for some it came relatively early in life, for others it came much later), they did not vacillate. They set themselves on a course of action—prayer and the works of charity—with uncommon zeal. The result was that eventually they manifested a greater degree of holiness, a greater dedication to the things of God, and a greater fidelity to their dedication than most people do.

But this dedication and strong sense of purpose did not make the saints "prayer-aholics," nor give them tunnel vision, nor produce antisocial fanatics. It did not make them dull, bland, humorless, faceless caricatures. Indeed, it was their strong dedication and their commitment to God that led them to undertake, and accomplish, those things that most people would not even think of doing.

How many people, for example, would try to organize a group of people to care for the poor, the sick, the widows, the orphans, and the alienated, as St. Vincent de Paul did when he gathered the men and women who later became the Vincentian Fathers and the Daughters of Charity? How many statesmen would face the problem of St. Thomas More, England's most famous Chancellor—a problem of conscience that would cost him his life—with such grace and good humor? How many could organize a whole school system for the poor without any financial aid from the state—and in the face of powerful opposition—and staff that system with volunteers (who later formed themselves into the religious congregation known as the Christian Brothers), as St. John de la Salle did? How many would leave home to establish Christian communities among native peoples as Junipero Serra and the North American Martyrs did? How many women, while raising a family alone, could organize a group of women into a religious community dedicated to educating the children of the poor, as Elizabeth Seton did in the United States in the early 1800s? No, the saints were not passive, holier-than-thou zealots. They were active doers, whose attachment to God and the quality of their spiritual life made them creative—and made

Saint Elizabeth Seton

the world better because they lived saintly lives.

Who Says They Are Saints?

The practice of remembering certain persons as being in special touch and having a special relationship with God is as old as the Church itself. The Apostles, and Jesus' mother Mary, of course, were honored for being "close to the Lord." As time went on and Christians were persecuted and some put to death for their faith, those who gave their lives—the martyrs—were remembered and honored. After the days of persecution, other people were recognized for leading lives of great holiness and were honored with the apostles and martyrs. About 1171 A.D., the right of declaring certain persons to be saints was reserved to the pope. (Before that, bishops and their people in various areas said that certain people were worthy of veneration and remembrance because of the holiness of their lives.) Eventually, the process of canonization now in use in the Church was established. In this way saints are presented to the whole Church for honor and veneration in a public ceremony. Canonization is a sign to all Christians that God's grace has once again triumphed over human limitations.

Why Pray to the Saints?

Saints are honored and their help is sought through prayer because of the Christian belief in life after earthly death. Christians on earth seek the help of those who have experienced earthly death because they believe that those living in the risen dimension of existence have not lost interest in or concern for the human affairs of the people on earth. In fact, they believe that their interest and concern have increased because of the new dimension of their vision of God's plan for people's salvation. *They believe that the saints continue to be God's instruments of grace on earth just as they were while they lived their limited, earthly lives.*

This interaction between those who have died and those who still live on earth is called "the communion of saints." It is the belief that there is a common bond existing among all members of the Church—the living and the dead—and that they have mutual interests, mutual concerns, and mutual love for each other.

What is the difference between a religious brother and a religious priest? Which is it better to be?

What is "All Saints Day"? When is it? Why does the Church recommend that children be given saints' names at baptism?

Who was Junipero Serra? Who were the North American Martyrs?

Select one religious order of men and one of women and be prepared to give a brief report on each.

Most religious identify their order or congregation with initials, like "OFM," "IHM," "FSC," and "SJ." Make a list of five religious congregations, giving their initials and indicating what the initials stand for.

Discuss the wisdom of going to "dangerous" countries to bring the Gospel and help the poor.

Conclusion

This keeping in touch with God is a very personal thing. As we mentioned previously, all Christians are called to be holy—to live lives of prayer and good works. But our holiness is to be ours, expressing our personal relationship with God by the quality of our active life and the intensity of our prayer life. We may or may not be called to the religious life, and we may or may not be called to extraordinary works of charity. We are all given the grace of God to live the kind of life God envisioned for us in His plan for His creation. We can fulfill our particular role in that plan if we keep in touch with God.

Prepare a brief report on each of two saints. Select one male and one female.

Summary

It is up to the individual to keep in touch with the God he or she believes in.

As the Son of God, Jesus revealed what God's plan for all people is. He brought Divine Life into creation.

Prayer is a response to the presence of God. Christian prayer is a response to the saving presence of God.

Jesus teaches all people to look on God as Father.

Certain Christians are called by God to express their Christianity in the religious life.

Saints are persons recognized for their goodness and holiness. Canonized saints are those declared so by the Church.

Words You Should Know

Be sure that you can define each of the words given below. If you are not sure of any, consult the Word List on page 234.

beatification	indiscriminate	specific
canonization	nondivine	transcendent
contemplative	philosophical	uniqueness
homage	relatively	vacillate
immanent	sophisticated	Western civilization

For Review, Discussion, Research, and Reflection

1. Summarize briefly the process by which people came to know God as Christians know Him.

2. What is the central belief of Christians?

3. What is the meaning of the resurrection of Christ?

4. Discuss why the Church, for most of her official prayers, uses "Through Christ our Lord" as an ending.

5. What is Christian prayer? Give the names of five commonly used Christian prayers.

6. Your book says a person ought to pray even when he or she doesn't feel like praying. What reason is given?

7. Christians speak of God's presence as "saving." Explain how God's presence is saving.

8. What does Jesus say God's relationship to people is like?

9. What do Catholic Christians mean by "the religious life"? What are religious orders or congregations a sign of in the Catholic Church?

10. What vows do most religious take when they join a religious community? Explain each.

11. Prepare a brief report on the history of the religious life as it is found in the Catholic Church.

12. What is a saint, as the term is now used in the Catholic Church? Why are some people canonized in the Church? Have any been canonized lately?

13. The Blessed Virgin is called "the universal saint of the Catholic Church." Can you give a reason for this? Can you name three different national shrines dedicated to the Blessed Virgin?

14. Discuss the differences between the saints who engaged in works of charity and people who devote their lives to works of charity in groups such as the Peace Corps and the Papal Volunteers.

15. Look up the name of two religious orders in a Catholic magazine or newspaper. Write to them asking for information so that you can participate in a kind of "religious fair."

16. To learn something of the art of contemplation, go off by yourself somewhere and give serious thought to some aspect of your religious life. Think seriously, perhaps, about God, or Jesus' resurrection, the role of Mary in salvation, the meaning of the Eucharist, heaven, eternal life, and so forth. You might find it profitable, too, to read one of the psalms carefully thinking of its meaning for you.

17. Have you ever thought about becoming a priest or a religious? Have you ever thought about being a saint? Both are ways of keeping in touch with God in a special way.

Christian Prayer As a Personal Response to God's Saving Presence

rev 2,3.
study

When you pray, do not be like the hypocrites! They love to stand up and pray in the houses of worship and on the street corners, so that everyone will see them. I assure you, they have already been paid in full. But when you pray, go to your room, close the door, and pray to your Father, who is unseen. And your Father, who sees what you do in private, will reward you.

—Matthew 6:5, 6

2.1 Moments of Prayer

As we said, when a person responds as an individual to God's presence, the response is called "Prayer." When a group of people respond in an official way to God's presence, it is called "The Liturgy." Both are natural to human beings and to the common human experience. Ever since the dawn of consciousness, people have prayed to whatever God is

for them, and they have worshipped this God as a group in an official group way.

Whether a person realizes it or not, God is at the very heart of existence. From His Being flows our being, our existence. It is to Him that our inner self, our spiritual self, our mysterious self is drawn, like metal to a magnet, by God Himself. That is why prayer is at once natural to a human being and very personal.

But a person's response to this call of God to his inner self is like his or her response to anything else. It depends on his or her awareness of the reality of the call. A deeply spiritual person is very conscious of the reality. For him, God's presence is a reality to which he responds fervently. A person who is not conscious of the reality of God's call to his inner self has little experience of the reality of God's presence. His response is weak, or, in some cases, completely lacking. In the one case, a person has a deep, trusting relationship with God. In the other, he has little, if anything to do with God.

If, as we said, prayer is a positive response to the reality of God's presence in our life, it is easy to see why we can say that prayer is you expressing your relationship with God as you live your life. Or, to put it another way, we can say that **prayer is an expression of faith.**

For those who are aware of the meaning of the presence of God, their entire life is a prayer because they are aware that God is present to them always and everywhere because they live in God's world (what other world is there?). *They respond to this presence in the way they live their lives.* In other words, they do what they do to the best of their ability and in the way they think God would have them to do it because God is present to them. Their actions are done for God and in His presence. This does not mean that they are actively thinking of God every minute of their day. It means that they live their ordinary lives with an attitude and a philosophy which is God-oriented, God-directed, and God-related.

For such people, conscious of the God-dimension of their lives, **prayer is constant** because everything they do is a prayer. Consider a mother, for example. She can go about her work (whatever it is) simply because she is aware that her life is God-ordained and can respond to that awareness by doing her work for God. Or take a father who goes to work every day to provide for his family. He can do it because he has to, because he likes to, because he is successful, because he wants "nice" things, or for a host of other reasons, good, bad, or indifferent. But if he goes to work, conscious of the God-aspect of life, he goes with a slightly different attitude from one who does not go with such an attitude. The work may be the same and the results similar, but one person goes along unconscious of the God-aspect of life and the other goes along conscious that God is acting in and through her or him for the good of others. For that person, life is a prayer, for he or she is responding to the presence of God in his or her life.

You, too, can respond to God's presence in your life as a student, a member of a family, an athlete, a musician, a scientist, a bag boy or checkout girl, or whatever. You can be pleasant, cheerful,

helpful, loyal, or committed because you do what you do in and for God. You don't have to, of course. It just makes whatever you are doing easier, more pleasant, and more personally profitable.

You must not confuse this aspect of prayer with affected piety, false religiosity, or "moments of prayer." Affected piety is phoney, cheap, and a falsehood. False religiosity can be either hypocritical (pretending to be religious) or pietistic (assuming an attitude of piety or devotion in whatever a person does). Neither is living in response to the presence of God. Both are in response to what other persons might think. Neither is prayer even though both might look like prayer.

"Moments of prayer" are those special times in one's life when a person deliberately and directly turns to God. They are those times when a person seeks out God, goes in search of Him, or tries to contact Him. "Moments of prayer" are a part of, but distinct from, a life lived in response to the presence of God. They are special or particular because a person turns his attention to God in a special or particular way. They can be times we set aside for prayer like before meals or at bedtime, during a school liturgy function or a class prayer-time, before a ball game, or at a public function. They can be spontaneous, arising in a moment of quiet or as a reaction to a beautiful scene, a moving situation, a thought implanted by a speaker. They can be caused by something we read, a happy circumstance of our life, or a moment of sorrow or tragedy. "Moments of prayer" can be short or long, they can occur anytime, in any place, and while a person is doing "other things."

There is nothing mysterious about these moments of prayer. Almost everyone experiences them, or sets aside special times for them. Such prayers arise spontaneously, or from some kind of felt need, or in response to a spiritual experience, or from the habit of prayer.

Give three examples of "moments of prayer."

Give two examples of affected piety or false religiosity.

Do you ever experience "moments of prayer"? Under what circumstances?

How are "moments of prayer" different from regularly scheduled times of prayer?

2.2 Kinds of Responses

These moments of prayer express four general kinds of response: petition, sorrow, thanksgiving, and adoration. **Adoration,** as the name implies, is a response to the awesome majesty of God. It is the first and most natural response of a person to the very thought of God. Almost all positive responses to God's presence bring out this sense of awe, wonder, and reverence. It is to this sense of God that Christians respond with the ancient prayer: "Glory be to the Father, and to the Son, and to the Holy Spirit, as it was in the beginning, is now, and shall be forever."

Prayers of thanksgiving are a second kind of response of people to the thought of God. When a person realizes that all things come from God, and that particular experiences of his life stem from God's care for him in particular—his talents, a moment of success, an answer to a prayer—his response is one of gratitude. It is to this sense of gratitude that Christians respond with prayers of thanks, such as the traditional prayer after meals. A vivid example of this kind of prayer, even in the face of hardship, appeared in the *Chicago Tribune:*

SACRAMENTO, Cal., Tami Hogan was a bright 9-year-old who always showed her parents her school work.

Except one item. It was a crayon illustrated poem called "Thank

You for Life" that she wrote herself. It said:

"Thank you Lord for letting me be alive today,
"I like to try to help in many ways,
"Thank you for my family,
"We always play together,
"We do live quite happily,
"Oh! Thank you for the sunshine weather,
"It's just wonderful to be alive!"

Tami's father, Gary, a lieutenant with the suburban Carmichael fire department, said he and his wife found the poem the day after his little girl died last Thursday of leukemia.

"My wife looked in a folder, and there was this poem right on top,"

he said. "We'd never seen it before. I wonder if she planned it that way."

Her father said he found out in December, 1970, that Tami had the deadly disease.

"We never told her that she had leukemia because we always hoped she'd become well again," Hogan said. "We just told her it was an infection.

"She was reserved, shy, and thoughtful. She was always concerned about everybody else, even at the last. The day she died she asked her mother how she—her mother—was doing."

Tami's teacher, Sister Mary Carton of Our Lady of the Assumption School, said the little girl knew something was wrong. "She said once she wished she could have just one day when she didn't feel sick."

Tami's grandmother, Mrs. Robert Mead, said the youngster "could put herself in your place. She knew more than what you thought she knew about life."

Funeral services will be held tomorrow. Tami's friends have established a scholarship fund in her name.*

A third kind of prayer people say in their moments of prayer is a **prayer of sorrow.** Prayers of sorrow are said in response to feelings of guilt for actions not worthy of us as human beings, or to actions that are sinful. They express an awareness of behavior that is not in the best interests of a particular person, of another person, or of society. They express a regret at having done an action that is contrary to one's own good, the good of another, or the good of the community in which one lives, works, recreates, or prays. They express a resolve to avoid such actions in the future.

Acts of sorrow, or contrition, are common among Christians. Most familiar to Catholics, of course, are the Act of Contrition said during the reception of the Sacrament of Reconciliation and the Penitential Formula said by the community assembled for Mass. Prayers of sorrow, of course, need not be formula prayers and should not be reserved only to the sacramental experience. They ought to be said after any act for which a person feels regret.

*© 1972, Chicago Tribune. Used with permission.

Prayers of petition, like prayers of adoration, thanksgiving, and sorrow, are a response to the very thought of God. They express a person's dependence on God, his or her need for God's help, and his or her confidence that God will help. They most perfectly express a person's understanding of the meaning of God's saving presence. That is, they express an awareness that the God of Christians is not a remote God, not an indifferent God, not a hostile God bent on vengeance. He is a God who is interested and involved in the affairs of His world.

Prayers of petition are an expression of humility. In asking God, a person admits his own helplessness, his own limited capabilities. Ultimately they are expressions of faith because they stem from a Christian's realization that God wants us to ask Him for things.

Nothing in the New Testament teaching on prayer comes through so clearly and forcibly as the teaching on prayers of petition. "Ask and you will receive,"

There are certain moments when whatever be the attitude of the body, the soul is on its knees.

Knock and the door will be opened to you. For everyone who asks will receive, and anyone who seeks will find, and the door will be opened to him who knocks" (Matthew 7:7, 8). He then goes on to ask, "Would any of you who are fathers give your son a stone when he asks for bread? Or would you give him a snake when he asks for a fish? As bad as you are, you know how to give good things to your children. How much more, then, will your heavenly Father give good things to those who ask him!" (Matthew 7:9–11).

St. Paul seems to summarize the New Testament teaching on prayers of petition in his Epistle to the Philippians. "May you always be joyful in your union with the Lord. I say it again; rejoice! Show a gentle attitude toward everyone. The Lord is coming soon. Don't worry about anything, but in all your prayers ask God for what you need, always asking him with a thankful heart" (4:4–6).

2.3 Mental Prayer

Most people think of prayer in terms of words spoken aloud or said silently. There is another kind of prayer, called mental prayer, or meditation, that takes place in the mind. It arises in the mind as a result of thinking about God or the things of God, about spiritual experiences, or from reflections on the Scripture or the liturgy. It may be, but oftentimes is not, separate from vocal prayer because the very nature of thinking about God elicits prayer formed into words.

Mental prayer differs essentially from vocal prayer in that mental prayer consists in thinking about God or the things of God first, and then praying. Vocal prayer, on the other hand, is a verbalized response to an experience, accompanied by thought on the meaning of what is being said. In addition, mental prayer differs from simply thinking about God, as you are doing now, in that the thinking results in prayer, not simply in the act of thinking or in conclusions drawn from the act of thinking. It is essentially prayer, not an intellectual exercise or effort.

Mental prayer is an act of reflection. It deepens our awareness of God, of the sacredness and religious nature of life, of our relationship with God, and of the meaning and direction of our life. It is a prayerful human activity that is centered on God and His Divine Activity in life. It is an interior reaching out for Mystery.

___

In your experience, what is the most common form of response to the saving presence of God? Why do you think it is the most common?

Name four things for which a person your age should thank God. Do you ever thank Him for them?

Do you think it is proper for an athlete, musician, or any performer to pray before a testing moment? Why? Why not? What do you think most people in such circumstances pray for?

Give one example of each kind of response mentioned above.

___

2.4 Special Forms of Prayer

In addition to the common responses to God's saving presence, there are special forms of response found rather commonly among Catholics. One of these is called "ejaculatory prayer." Another is called "charismatic prayer." A third is a form of worship or personal prayer directed to a Divine Being, a mystery of faith, a particular aspect of Jesus' life, or to a special person like the Blessed Virgin. These are called "devotions."

The word "ejaculatory" is used for what some have called "those quick thrusts of prayer."* They are short phrases or sentences like "God love you," "Jesus, Mary, Joseph," "O God," "St. Anthony help me find that ring," and so forth. Like javelins, ejaculatory prayers are thrown toward heaven.

Charismatic prayer is the prayer of Christians who feel that they have personally experienced a coming of the Holy Spirit into their lives. It is a more spontaneous and less formal form of prayer which expresses one's personal experience of God's love. It is often characterized by praying "in tongues" (languages other than one's native or known language).

The natural inclination people have to particularize prayer has given rise, in Catholic circles, to many kinds of "devotions."

It is true that Christian prayer is a positive response to a person's awareness of the presence of God in his or her life and is directed specifically to God as God. It is also true that people seem to have a need to focus their prayer on a particular aspect of the Mystery of God as this mystery is understood in Christianity. This we learn from Jesus himself who taught us to pray to God as Father.

What particular aspect of the Mystery of God a person focuses on in a particular

*From the Latin word *ejaculatus* meaning shot out, thrown quickly, or thrusted.

prayer or act of devotion depends on the person's understanding, personal desire or inclination, cultural upbringing, and specific need. It may also arise from a specific liturgical season (such as Easter), a particular religious feast (such as Corpus Christi), or a particular holy day or holiday (such as Christmas or the Fourth of July). Or it may arise from a particular time and place (such as the celebration of a patron saint in a parish).

The principal devotions in the Catholic Church are those associated with Christ, such as devotion to the Blessed Sacrament in the form of Benediction, Forty Hours, or visits to the reserved Species. Second in importance are devotions to the Blessed Virgin, such as the Rosary, the May and October devotions, the various feasts of Mary celebrated during the Church year, or national feasts of Mary (such as the Immaculate Conception in the United States, Our Lady of Fatima in Portugal, or Our Lady of Guadalupe in Mexico). Next come devotions to national saints, such as St. George in England, and devotions to specific saints among particular nationalities, such as St. Joseph among the Polish and St. Patrick among the Irish. After that are devotions to patron saints, such as parish saints or name-sake patrons like John or Barbara and devotions to particular saints, such as St. Thomas Aquinas, patron of studies, St. Thomas More, patron of lawyers, and St. Cecelia, patroness of musicians.

Devotional prayers take on many forms. Sometimes they are private. Sometimes they are public, for example, the processions and prayers at Lourdes. Sometimes they are paraliturgical. Sometimes they are civic, for example, the Holy Week observances in South American towns and villages. Whatever their forms, they are very much a part of *the human experience of prayer.* They engulf the whole person in the act of prayer: body, mind, heart, emotions, and the need for expression and community.

There is a danger, of course, in any devotional practice of prayer. It can become very narrow if the devotion blinds one to other forms of prayer or to the object of prayer, God. It can become obsessive if it is the only form of prayer, or becomes overritualized or stereotyped, or if it is practiced through fear or scrupulosity. It can become foolish if it takes on magic or near-magic qualities. But devotional prayer, rightly engaged in, can be a genuine force in a person's life, leading to a deeper spiritual life, a more personal relationship with God, and a greater participation in the liturgical worship of the whole Church.

What particular devotion are you most familiar with?

What devotion do you practice most often? Why?

Do you ever use ejaculatory prayers? Which ones?

If you have any experience with devotions of other nationalities or places, exchange your experiences with your classmates.

Read thoughtfully either Psalm 150 or John 14 and 15; then meditate on what each is saying, allowing yourself to pray spontaneously as you meditate.

2.5 Some Characteristics of Personal Prayer

As we have said, for those who believe in God, **prayer is natural.** It is a normal response to the acceptance of the idea of God. If a person truly believes in God, he can no more not-respond than he can not-breathe. (Even not responding is a response, isn't it, like not liking someone is a response to that person?) But if a person truly believes God is present, he or she will seek Him out, naturally.

It's like searching out a friend. If you want to contact him, you go looking for him. You call him on the phone, or you go where you'll most likely find him. So it is with God. *Prayer is going to God.* You know where He is—you make contact with Him. It's as much a part of your human nature as eating or sleeping. If you are a religious person, prayer is natural to you. (But that does not mean that it's always easy, just as eating and sleeping are not always easy.)

Because prayer is natural, it will vary, as we have said, according to circumstances of time and place. How you pray will depend on your mood, your need, and your awareness of the God-dimension of your life. For that reason, **prayer is spontaneous.** It is a response to the situation which calls forth the prayer. It reflects the mood, the feeling, and the reason for prayer. Like other responses in life, prayer may be happy or sad, anxious or calm, full of assurance, expressing wonder or awe, adoration, or thanksgiving. It may be vocal or silent, deeply meditative or light-hearted and simple. It may be the thoughtful recitation of a prayer made up by others, or it may be a prayer you work up for yourself.

Whatever its form, your prayer must express how you feel and what your awareness is at the moment. Your prayer must reflect you. To properly reflect you, your thoughts and the words you use (if you use any) should be those which come to your mind, arising from the situation, your mood, and your understanding of what God is for you. *Your words, your ideas, and your feelings expressed in prayer should form your prayer.*

This aspect of personal prayer is very well illustrated in Robert Hale's "A Prayer for Peace," found in *The Franciscan Message* (February, 1972):

> Lord,
> forgive us for polluting our planet
> and hanging a mushroom-shaped
>   cloud
> in the heavens.

As we look up at this cloud,
may we learn the lessons of
    history:
that an arms race has always led
    to war
or economic ruin.

Forgive us our progress
that has led us to more powerful
    weapons
and impersonal ways of killing.

The airman
who drops a bomb from 30,000
    feet
cannot feel the pangs of
    conscience
as strongly as a man
who stabs a bayonet into his
    brother.

Forgive us
for manufacturing the instruments
    of death:
bacteriological,
radiological, and other
illogical weapons,

which can cause plagues worse
    than the Middle Ages,
poison our current enemy's water
    supplies,
and kill each person 100 times.

May we, instead,
forge the instruments of peace:
tractors instead of tanks,
medicines instead of missiles,
schools instead of submarines,

In the name of the Prince of
    Peace. Amen.

Even in ritual prayers like those you say at Mass, your words must express your thoughts and your understanding of what the ritual form is saying. The so-called "emptiness" of ritual prayers or "formula" prayers is not due to the formula (which is usually very rich in meaning). It is due to how they are said, or to the routine or thoughtlessness which accompanies them.

When it is spontaneous, **prayer is thoughtful.** It cannot help but be thoughtful because our minds are occupied with it. Unfortunately, what often passes for prayer—that is, the almost-thoughtless repetition of formulas—is not really prayer. A person's mind is not on what he or she is saying. Such a "prayer" is not done in response to the presence of God, and certainly is not "searching Him out." It is a response to a duty or to a social convention. It's like going to class on a hot day. You may be present in body, but, unless you are very interested in the subject or the teacher is very good, your mind can be a thousand miles away.

True prayer, like involvement in anything, requires attention—the mind must be on what we are doing. That is why there is danger in confining our prayers to set formulas and never praying spontaneously. If we always use set formulas (like "The Lord's Prayer" or the standard "Grace before Meals"), we

There is no one way to pray.
Prayer is too wide, too individual, too personal,
and too God-linked to have any final definition.
In its final analysis, prayer can be talked about,
but it also must be experienced.
It must be entered into.
Words are not enough;
contemplation of God is necessary.
Otherwise prayer is only words.

can fall into a routine of recitation, be easily distracted, and only spend time "at praying" without ever really praying.

That does not mean to say, however, that we must never use formula prayers. Sometimes spontaneous prayer can be difficult, as in moments of great sorrow, or on an occasion when we really don't know how to respond adequately. This is one of the reasons that the Church has formula prayers for such occasions as death. They help people over a difficult moment and help them express their faith-concepts without having to struggle for ideas. Incidentally, the formulas of prayer in use in most churches were originally spontaneous—they grew out of the mood, the feeling, and the situation. The faith-community felt that they expressed well what the community felt when they were composed.

Discuss the pluses and minuses in the use of formula prayers and in the use of spontaneous or "made up" prayers.

Select any two of the following situations and, on a separate sheet of paper, write a short prayer illustrating the characteristics of personal prayer.

—Your best friend is critically ill with pneumonia.

—You read of an earthquake in a Central American town.

—Your team is playing for the championship.

—You are asked to write the opening prayer for a Mass during Lent.

—You are asked to deliver the closing prayer at a day of recollection.

—You have just been elected president of your class.

—Your grandmother asks you to say grace before meals at her fiftieth wedding anniversary.

2.6 God's Response to Prayer

Prayers of adoration, thanksgiving, and sorrow are relatively easy because they are natural responses to a person's awareness of God's presence. Prayers of petition are easy, too, most of the time, because it is usually not hard to ask for things we want. But prayers of petition can pose a problem for many people because, sooner or later, due to the disappointment they have experienced with such prayers, the question, "Will (or how does) God answer prayers?" arises.

The question is natural. It is the question of a maturing mind, and it is God's way of leading people to a more mature prayer life. The answer to the question is not so simple. What we can say, of course, is that if God is God, He can answer our prayers and does. How He does is another matter.

Sometimes God's answer is immediate and visible, as in the attested miracles of

If I worship you, Lord, will you give me peace of mind?

. . . and fame, and success in business?

. . . and give a personal, written guarantee of immortality for me and my family?

such places as Lourdes, and in the common experience of those who have prayed. (Who has prayed and not experienced an answer to at least some of his or her prayers?) Sometimes the answer is given through the work of others. Take the case of prayers for the sick. Most often these prayers are answered through the skill of doctors and nurses, or through the work of scientists producing medicines, or through the care and attention the sick get from those who love them.

Sometimes God answers prayers by bringing about a change of attitude in the one praying. He will not, for example, generally produce a new eye damaged in an accident, but He will help the person praying to accept the affliction and give the person a peace of mind that was not there, perhaps, before the prayer.

Sometimes prayers are answered over a long period of time, through changes which happen so gradually, so naturally, that if we were not alert to the change, we would not recognize it as an answer to prayer. And sometimes God answers prayers with a "no." He knows that what

is asked is not really for the best. He knows that it is only an attempt to impose a person's desire on God or on His plan for creation.

However prayers of petition are answered, they are answered. God does want to help us. With this in mind, people who pray for things should ask with confidence. They should pray with trust that God will respond to their prayers.

But, truly believing that God will respond to our prayers of petition is, perhaps, the most difficult of all the aspects of prayer. It becomes increasingly easy to pray spontaneously and thoughtfully as our prayer-life develops, but it is not easy to be confident—really trusting—at the beginning of our mature prayer-life (and off and on throughout our mature prayer-life). Many times, we expect an instant response or mini-miracle, or we get the feeling that whatever happens is going to happen anyway, prayer or no prayer. *And this is where trust comes in.* If we knew exactly how and when prayers were going to be "answered," there would be no trust. There would be automation: we'd put in our required amount and get back our favorite answer.

Oh—I must worship you "because you are God"?

What kind of a deal is that?

God does not hand out responses like a gumball dispenser! He is not a robot or a programmed prayer responder!

Confidence in prayer depends upon our realization that the purpose of prayer is not simply to ask for things we cannot get otherwise. Its purpose is to enable us to contact God. Confidence also depends upon our realization that prayers of request are answered in God's time and God's way. God does not answer prayers of request with a stupendous show. His ways are often hidden and mysterious, and often so quiet and unobtrusive that we might miss them if we do not consciously look for them. Many times, too, God does not respond to prayers of request exactly as we want Him to. He responds in the way that is best for the individual and the common good of all people.

What kind of a world would it be if God responded with some kind of "miracle" at every hasty prayer? Suppose that you were playing golf and you hit a bad shot sure to go into the water. As you saw it headed for disaster you shouted a prayer to God and He suddenly made the ball veer away or go over the water in defiance of the laws of physics. Great for you! But suppose it happened to your opponent?

Our confidence that our prayer will be answered stems from our faith. If we truly believe in a saving God, we know that He is acting in our lives, is listening to us, and is responding to our requests because He is our Father. "Those who are led by God's Spirit," says St. Paul in his Epistle to the Romans, "are God's sons. For the Spirit that God has given you does not make you slaves and cause you to be afraid; instead, the Spirit makes you God's children, and by the Spirit's power we cry out to God, 'Father! my Father!' God's Spirit joins himself to our spirits to declare that we are God's children. Since we are his children, we will possess the blessings he keeps for his people, and we will also possess with Christ what God has kept for him . . ." (8:14–17).

Have you ever felt like it was useless to pray? When? Why do you suppose you felt that way?

How to Live

Live each day to the fullest. Get the most from each hour, each day, and each age of your life. Then you can look forward with confidence, and back without regrets.

Be yourself — but be your best self. Dare to be different and to follow your own star. And don't be afraid to be happy. Enjoy what is beautiful. Love with all your heart and soul. Believe that those you love, love you.

Forget what you have done for your friends, and remember what they have done for you. Disregard what the world owes you, and concentrate on what you owe the world.

When you are faced with a decision, make that decision as wisely as possible — then forget it. The moment of absolute certainty never arrives.

And above all, remember that God helps those who help themselves. Act as if everything depended upon you, and pray as if everything depended upon God.

S. H. Payer

Do you *think* God answers prayers?
Do you *know* if He does? Do you
believe He does? What is the
difference in each case?

Can you give an instance from your
own life that your prayers were
answered? Explain.

When Pope John Paul II was shot,
people from all over the world
prayed that God would spare his life
and that he would recover. How did
God answer these prayers?

You are familiar with the Prayers of
the Faithful said after the homily at
Sunday Mass. Make up three sample
prayers that would apply to your life
and the life of your peer group now.

Conclusion

Everyone knows that he or she ought to
pray, but how many do, on a regular
basis? For many, prayer is not easy, but
like anything worthwhile, it is worth
doing. The nice thing about it is, prayer
becomes easier as we learn to pray.

Summary

People who understand the presence of
God in their lives live in the presence of
God in everything they do.

Everyone should make sure that there
are prayer times in his or her life.

A person's response to God's presence
might be one of awe, thanksgiving, sorrow, or asking for help.

There are many different kinds of prayers: vocal and mental; ejaculatory, charismatic, and devotional; private and
public; personal and liturgical; formal
and informal; formula or spontaneous.

Prayers ought to be said with attention
and confidence.

Because God is God, prayers can be and
will be answered. Only the way they are
answered is in doubt.

Words You Should Know

Be sure that you can define the words given below. If there are any you cannot define, look them up in the Word List on page 234.

hypocrite
paraliturgical
religiosity

ritual
scrupulous

spontaneous
verbalize

For Review, Discussion, Research, and Reflection

1. You have already had one general definition for prayer. In this topic, two particular definitions are given. Be sure that you can give each from memory.

2. Distinguish between what your book calls "constant prayers" and "moments of prayer."

3. Select three different people in three different kinds of jobs and suggest how they can make their lives a "constant prayer."

4. Are there any kinds of lives that cannot be "constant prayers"? Why? Why not?

5. Name and explain the four kinds of response to God's presence expressed in prayer.

6. What reasons does your book give for prayers of petition?

7. How can a person avoid having his or her formula or routine prayers be simply word repetitions and not true prayers?

8. Father Simon Tugwell, a Dominican priest says: "If we are too bored to listen to our own prayers, is there any reason to think that God will find them any less boring?" Discuss what he meant by that in light of your own common experience of prayer.

9. Discuss why most people feel uncomfortable when asked to pray aloud not using formula prayers.

10. If someone said to you that they don't pray because God doesn't answer prayers, what would your response be?

11. What do the following words of writer Alfred Tennyson say to you: "More things are wrought by prayer than this world dreams of. . . . For what are men better than sheep or goats that nourish a blind life within the brain, if, knowing God, they lift not hands of prayer both for themselves and those who call them friends?"

12. Two basketball teams from Catholic schools are playing for the championship. Each team is led in prayer for victory by the team captain. Discuss first whether this is right, and second how God answers such prayers.

13. What is mental prayer? How does it differ essentially from vocal prayer? How does it differ from mere reflection?

14. Why do devotions seem to be an integral part of a person's prayer life?

15. A common Catholic private devotion is saying what is called a "Morning Offering." Prepare a short, suitable Morning Offering that would reflect your own views and needs.

16. Prepare a report on the devotions practiced at the shrine of Our Lady of Lourdes or some similar shrine in the Christian world.

17. What ought to be the two principal characteristics of personal prayer? Explain each.

18. St. Clement said that prayer is conversation with God. Discuss what he meant by that.

19. On your way home from school today meditate on God's greatness. Reflect on the world around you, the immensity of the universe, and God's care for people. As you think, let your prayer rise spontaneously from what you are thinking.

20. In a book of familiar quotations look up the section on prayers. Read what is given, then pick out two that you like and be prepared to explain to the class why you like them.

The Liturgy Is the Catholic Church's Response to God's Saving Presence

For the liturgy, "through which the work of our redemption is accomplished" . . . is the outstanding means whereby the faithful may express in their lives, and manifest to others, the mystery of Christ and the real nature of the true Church. . . . While the liturgy daily builds up those who are within into a holy temple of the Lord, into a dwelling place for God in the Spirit, to the mature measure of the fullness of Christ, at the same time, it . . . shows forth the Church . . . as a sign lifted up among nations. . . .

—Constitution on the Sacred Liturgy

3.1 What Is the Liturgy?

Do you find it hard to keep your mind on what is happening at Mass? Do you sometimes wonder why you're there? Do you ever wish you were somewhere else? Everybody does now and again. Why, then, do people come together for the Mass?

It's natural.

Think of it this way. Human beings like to get together. They like to do things together. They work together to produce things. They join causes to bring about

change. They rally together to help people in trouble. They come together to express common concerns, to celebrate, and to share.

Religious people who come together share their awareness of the presence of God and respond to that awareness as a group. That is, they pray together when the occasion calls for it.

Like individual prayer, group prayer is natural, thoughtful, and confident, but it cannot generally be as spontaneous as individual prayer except in unusual circumstances. Like individual prayer, group prayer can be long or short, formal or informal. It can occur anytime or in any place. Like individual prayer, group prayer should reflect the mood of the group, and the circumstances and situation in which the group finds itself. Group prayer can be happy or sorrowful, thankful or petitionary, adoring, or begging for forgiveness for group failings.

People pray together for a number of different reasons. When they pray as a group of individuals sharing a common situation like a meal, a party, an election, a disaster, or an experience of God, the group prayer is public. When a group comes together as members of a particular Church and prays in the official, formal, ritual expression of the Church's worship, the group prayer is liturgical.

Although liturgical prayer is public, it differs from ordinary public prayer in that it is the official, public worship a particular religious group offers to its God as a group. It is an expression of the belief of the group, not only in God's presence, but in the kind of presence God has for the group. This is one of the reasons for the difference in liturgies as found in various religions.

3.2 The Catholic Liturgy Is a Celebration

For Catholics, the liturgy is a celebration of God's saving actions in Christ. It is a celebration because through its solemn, public, liturgical actions the Church is responding to what it believes God has done for people in His becoming a man in the person of Jesus. The Church expresses joy, happiness, and gratitude with appropriate ceremonies, giving visible appreciation of what something is or means, and of what Someone is or has done.

The liturgy is solemn (which, incidentally does not mean sad, somber, or gloomy) because it is serious, deeply earnest, and deals with a sublime or very important occasion, event, and Person. In other words, the liturgy is in keeping with what is being celebrated.

But what does the Church believe God has done in Christ that ought to be celebrated? Among other things, the Church in its liturgy celebrates:

God's creating people in His own image, that is, giving them intelligence and making it possible for them to participate in His creative act by developing themselves and the earth to bring both to their created goal.

—God's saving people from nondivine existence by sharing His Divine Life with them by becoming a man in the person of Jesus.

—God's making Himself visibly present to people in the person of Jesus.

91

—His demonstrating His purpose in creation through the meaning of Jesus' resurrection.

—His continued presence among people in His Church, Christ's visible body to the world.

—His dynamic creativity in the world through the action of Christ's Spirit, the Holy Spirit.

—His sharing His life fully with people in what we call eternity.

In other words, the Church in its liturgy celebrates God's saving presence in the lives of people. It invites its members to be a part of this celebration.

Name four different occasions in which people pray in public that the prayer is not liturgical.

—Is the liturgy a celebration for you? Why? Why not?

—Can the liturgy be a celebration if it is solemn? Why? Why not?

—What would you suggest be done to make the liturgy more of a celebration for you?

In the quotation that opens this topic, the term "Mystery of Christ" is used. What does it mean?

Be prepared to discuss the following questions in an open forum:

—Is the liturgy thought of as a celebration by most people? Why? Why not?

Take some time to read and think about that quotation. In an exchange of ideas with your classmates discuss the quotation until you come to an understanding of what it says.

3.3 The Catholic Liturgy Is a Sign and a Reality

Your whole life is influenced, even lived, by signs and symbols.* You judge the mood of your teacher, for example, by the way he or she looks or acts even before he or she says anything. You know what the penalty in a football or basketball game is by the signal the referee gives. You are guided along the road by lines, letters, and signals. You know what a double line means, what a highway sign tells you, and what a flashing light wants you to know. The logo of a TV station tells you what the network is. A football team's helmet sign and color tell you something about the team and what it thinks of itself. Its sign is its symbol.

So it is with most things in life, including religion. All religions have signs and symbols that have special meaning for those who believe. Because they deal with religion, however, they are considered sacred and holy. They are more than simply signs or symbols. They are special signs and symbols. The Jewish Star of David, for example, or the Mecca of Islam, or the Ganges River for Hindus are sacred and holy. They may be just

a star or a building, or a river to most people. But to those for whom they are religious signs or symbols, they are full of meaning. They symbolize, or point to, or stand for something beyond the things themselves. They point to, or mean something sacred, something mysterious, something religiously special.

Catholic liturgy, too, has signs, symbols, and special rituals that signify something special and sacred. The sign of the Cross, for example, is known as "the sign of a Christian." And when a person blesses himself or herself, it is usually taken to mean that that person is a Catholic. You are familiar with holy water, a genuflection, a bowed head, and the handshake during Mass. You have seen the priest's vestments, the paschal candle, blessings, anointings, statues, and the Way of the Cross. There are, literally, hundreds of

---

* A sign is any means, mark, figure, token, indication, or gesture used to convey an idea, indicate a place or action, or to point to something else. Traffic lights, arrows, kisses, and so forth are signs. A symbol is anything used to represent, stand for or in place of, or mean something else. The *x* in algebra, a wedding ring, and the American flag are symbols standing for a number, eternal love, and the ideals of America, respectively.

Common Signs and Symbols
Used in Catholic Liturgy

Sign of the cross
Wedding ring
Pascal candle
Incense
Concelebration
Priest raising host and chalice
Hands in prayer
Genuflection
Baptismal font
Church building
Priest wearing stole
Sign of peace

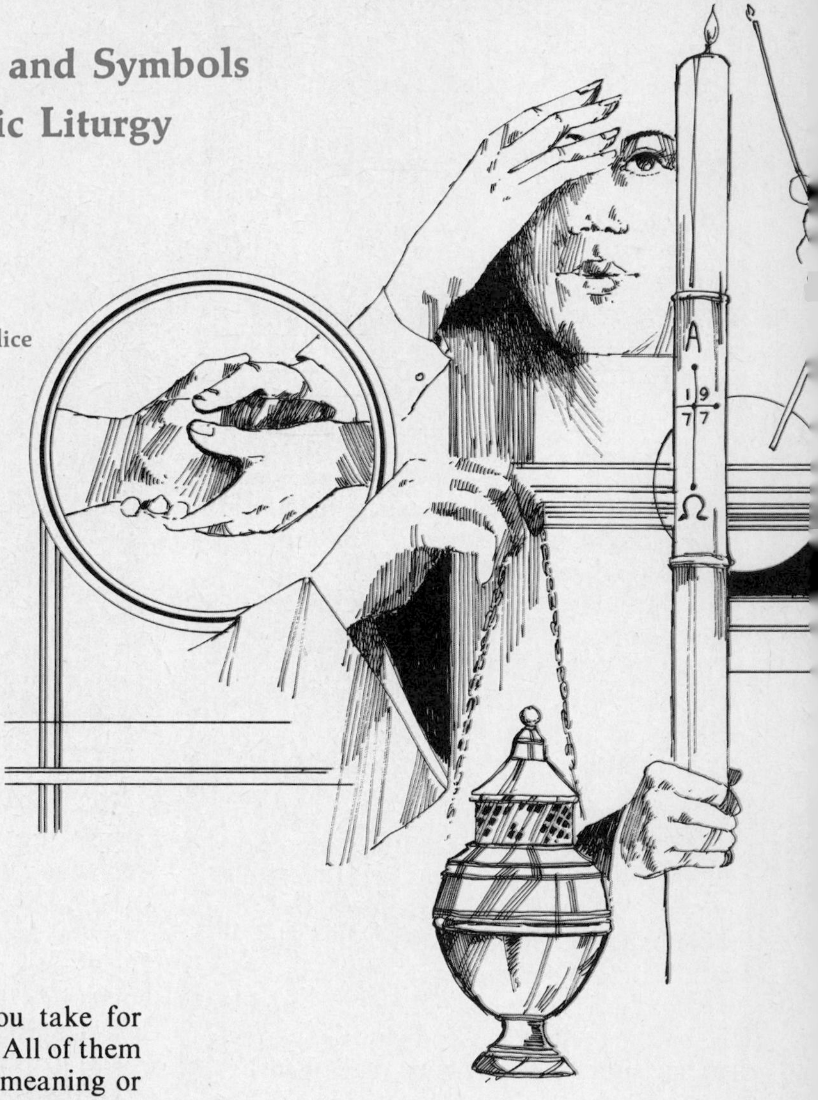

others signs and symbols you take for granted in your Catholic life. All of them signify something and have meaning or point to something beyond themselves.

The liturgy itself is a sign. It is a visible expression of God's saving actions in the Church. It is more than a sign, however. It is an act expressing the *reality* of God's saving actions in Christ. It is what it signifies. The Mass, for example, is not just a celebration of the presence of Jesus in the Church. It is not, either, just a celebration of his saving death and resurrection. It is also a visible expression

of that presence, death, and resurrection. Ordination is not only a sign that a person belongs to the official, public ministry of the Church. It is also the action through which a person actually becomes an official, public minister of the Church.

This is why the liturgy is so important—and so important for you. It is not simply a sacred, or holy, or religious action that you do or watch. It is God acting in your life as a saving God. It is God in the process of saving you—of making you holy. The action itself, and the words and actions of the act are signs of that reality. You need to look beyond the act itself to what it signifies and is. Then you'll see and appreciate its importance in your life.

The fact that a person cannot read a sign or does not know what it means does not make it a "nonsign." It merely means that the person, for whatever reason, does not understand the sign or appreciate it for what it is. This is one of the reasons you have to take a "Signs of the Road" test when trying for your driver's license. Some people's lack of awareness of the sign aspect of the sacraments might be compared to an American tourist's lack of awareness of the meaning of signs, say, in China or Japan. The signs are very meaningful for the Chinese or the Japanese. For an American they are almost totally incomprehensible.

3.4 Symbols and Rituals Are Important

Because a liturgical action is a sign, it must signify what it means. It is not enough to say that it is a sign, or that it means what we want it to mean. *It means what it is.* The Eucharist, for example, is not a meal, say, of a breakfast club or even a meal of good fellowship among Catholics. It has a special meaning—the meaning that Jesus gave it. While it is correct to say that the Eucharist is truly a meal, it is not just any meal. It is a meal in which the Risen Jesus is present sacramentally under the appearances of bread and wine.

Because the liturgy is a sign that must signify what it means, its symbols and rituals (what it celebrates with and how it celebrates) must have meaning also.* In other words, what is used in the celebration and what is said and done must also signify what the liturgical action is and means. That is why the Church has always been careful to say what the symbols are and what the actions must be. They must signify the meaning Jesus gave to them. If liturgical actions were done any way at all, or were left up to the whim of individuals, there would soon be so many confusing things going on that the liturgical action would have no significance at all. It would not signify God's action or have the meaning it ought to have. It would confuse those present. There would be no meaning for them at all.

Consider the symbolism of some of the sacraments. For example, in Baptism, the Church specifies using water. The reason? Water signifies life and cleansing. The celebration of Baptism signifies "new life" (the life of God and the life of the Church) and "cleansing" (abandoning old habits—cleansing oneself of habits of sin). What would be the symbolism of using, say, Pepsi Cola or orange juice? To be sure, you can think of *some* symbolism, but is it the symbolism of the sacrament as the Church understands Baptism?

By specifying the things used, the things said, and the things done, the Church not only preserves the symbolism of her liturgical actions. It also preserves the meaning, continuity, universality, and dignity of the symbol. In so doing, the Church preserves the meaning of the liturgical action as the Church understands this meaning.

But the symbolism and the ritual prescribed are not intended to be rigid and totally unvaried, as if the entire meaning were only in the thing itself. The basic symbolism is retained in the material used. The action done, within reason, can be flexible. That is why, for example, there are various rituals for celebrating Mass. Ritual (or the actions performed and the words used), you see, makes the symbols visible and meaningful. Both contribute to the sign-value of the liturgical action itself.

---

*Rituals are authorized ways of doing something, especially religious actions. When a person is baptized, for example, what is done is done in keeping with general rules for baptism laid out by those in authority to make rules for the liturgy. The purpose of the rules is to make sure the action does what it is supposed to do.

The solemn, official, public liturgy of the Church is, however, not only a sign of God's saving actions in and of itself for the members of the Church. It is also a sign to the world. It is visible evidence of the Church's dedication to things religious. It is visible evidence of God's acting in and through His Church for the good of the world and of the individual Church member's relationship to God. It is God's way of making His actions visible and available to everyone.

Can you name any other signs commonly used in the Church which are not directly associated with the liturgy?

Much of your life is lived in response to signs and symbols. On another sheet of paper or in the space provided, reproduce four different kinds of signs you are familiar with, and, after each, tell what it signifies.

You are generally familiar with the sacraments of the Catholic Church. Reflect on them for a few moments, then discuss what the sign and symbols of each might be except Baptism and the Eucharist.

On pages 94–95 are pictures of some common symbols in use in the Catholic Church. Select any four and tell what each symbolizes.

3.5 The Catholic Liturgy Is a Response of the Church

One more thing needs to be understood if the liturgy is to become really meaningful for you. The liturgy is not the action of an individual in relation to God (this is private prayer), nor is it the action of a group in relation to God (this is public prayer). It is the action of "The Body of Christ"—the Church as the visible sign of Christ in the world. *In other words, the liturgy is Christ acting specifically and particularly through his body (the Church) as he acted through his physical body during his visible, physical life on earth.*

For those who understand this, three things follow. First, the liturgy is the action of Christ and not the action of an individual. Therefore, the action must say what it means to the whole Church and not what someone or several might want it to mean or to express.

The second is that the liturgy does not have to conform to the needs or meet the daily changes of mood of the individual. It is not an individual action. It is an action of the Church. Therefore, it must meet the needs of the Church by responding to the meaning of Jesus for the whole Church.

The third is that because the liturgy is an action of Christ directed to God, it must be celebrated with fitting reverence, taste, decorum, and dignity whether it is celebrated in a church, a home, or in the open (as Mass is, for example, for soldiers in the field). Everything that is said and done, and everything that is used in a liturgical action should reflect this reverence and dignity. It should appear in the words and actions of the minister and the people. It should be reflected in the music, in the prayers, in the gestures, in the dress, in the responses, and in the movements. It should be evident in the place and in the materials used—the altar, the liturgical utensils, the candles, and the like. Should not all these things reflect the order and beauty of the liturgy? Are they not signs of our respect for and relationship with our all-holy God?

If this is understood, a person would not attend Mass, or a baptism, or a wedding in a careless, frivolous manner or for what he can get out of it emotionally (this is a narrow, selfish view of the nature of any liturgical action). He should not go simply because he feels like it. **He attends a liturgical action and participates actively in it because of what it is.**

On the other hand, a person does not avoid going to Mass (or a baptism or wedding) because he "doesn't get anything out of it" or because he "doesn't feel like it." Both indicate an almost total lack of understanding of how God has chosen to act in the world. The liturgy is not meant to be an emotional experience (though it certainly can be), and it is not waiting on our feelings for its expression.

Our participation in the Liturgy expresses our understanding of the mystery of Christ.

The liturgy is Christ acting—carrying out the purpose of his becoming a man and acting as savior in the history of people. God chose to express Himself in the person of Jesus at a particular time and in a particular place in history. He now chooses to manifest Himself in the Body of Christ and make Himself present to people in the actions of His Church: the liturgy.

In and through the Church, Christ is acting in the world of people—whether any particular individual believes it or not. If we wish to participate with Christ, if we wish to express our relationship to God liturgically, we need to participate in the action of Christ in the liturgy. This is its meaning.

Conclusion

So many Catholics attend the liturgy out of a sense of duty or obligation. So many feel that they don't get anything out of it. So many think that they are paying their dues to God by going to Church occasionally or attending a religious service.

This is unfortunate. For them, the rich symbolism, the deep meaning, the response-nature of the liturgy, and the spiritual mystery is lost. For them, the liturgy is not expressing a relationship with God. It is not a deeply rewarding spiritual experience. It is not a sign of Christ acting in the world to save it. It is not Christ acting in their lives as he acted during his physical life on earth. All this is because they do not understand what the liturgy really is. That, too, is unfortunate.

Summary

The liturgy is more than group prayer. It is the response of the Church to its awareness of what God is.

The liturgy is a sign of Christ acting in his Church.

The liturgy is a celebration of Christ's saving actions.

The Catholic liturgy is both a sign of God acting and the reality of that acting.

Because of what it is, the liturgy should be done with reverence and dignity.

Words You Should Know

Be sure that you can define the words given below. If there are any you are not sure of, look them up in the Word List on page 234.

decorum	liturgy	sign
frivolous	logo	symbol
incomprehensible	ritual	

For Review, Discussion, Research, and Reflection

1. What is liturgical prayer? How does it differ from public, group prayer? Are the prayers of the Pope on TV liturgical prayer? Why? Why not?

2. Give four examples of public, group prayer. Which ones have you participated in? What was done in each?

3. In a brief essay, tell what the Church celebrates in the liturgy.

4. Explain what you understand by the term "sign" as it is used in this book.

5. What is the liturgy a sign of? Explain what this means.

6. What is the meaning of the terms *ritual* and *symbol* as they are used in connection with the liturgy? Give an example of each.

7. What must a symbol "do"? Why?

8. Be prepared to discuss in an open forum whether or not your parish should direct its Sunday liturgy exclusively to persons your age so that they will participate more in the liturgy.

9. In a short written statement complete this idea: "A person ought to go to Mass because. . . ."

10. Explain the central thought contained in the section of this chapter entitled, "Christian liturgy is a response of the Church."

11. Check off which of the following liturgical actions you have participated in. When you have finished, be prepared to say whether or not the words and actions carried the meaning of the ceremony through to you.

Baptism

Confirmation

The Eucharist

The Ordination of a priest and/or deacon

The Sacrament of Reconciliation

The Sacrament of the Sick

The Wedding Ceremony

12. Find out what you can about symbols and signs used in the churches of your non-Catholic friends.

13. Discuss whether or not it is possible in today's busy world for Catholic families to engage in family prayer services. If you think it possible, suggest some ways for families to do so.

Part Two

Expressing a Relationship with God through the Liturgy

A Special Kind of
Relationship

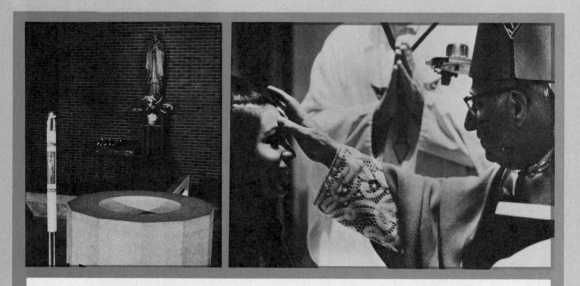

Every liturgical celebration, because it is an action of Christ the priest and of his body which is the Church, is a sacred action surpassing all others; no other action of the Church can equal its efficacy by the same title and to the same degree . . . the liturgy is the summit toward which the activity of the Church is directed; at the same time it is the fount from which all her power flows. . . . From the liturgy, therefore . . . grace is poured forth upon us; and the sanctification of men in Christ and the glorification of God . . . is achieved. . . .

—Constitution on the Sacred Liturgy

4.1 How God Acts in His Church

As we have said, Catholics respond to God's saving presence as individuals and as a Church group. The official, public Church response is called the liturgy. The liturgy expresses a particular kind of response and establishes a special kind of relationship. This special kind of relationship comes about because of the way God acts in the liturgy.

God acts in His Church in many ways. He uses the very existence of His Church, for example, to express His special and specific presence in the world. He uses it as a reminder of His presence,

as a kind of advertisement of His reality. He uses it as a voice opposing the secularism and sinfulness of the world. He uses it as a beacon light drawing attention to the reality that people's dreams for peace, goodness, and holiness can be achieved. He uses it to bring about social justice, calling His people to care for the poor, the sick, the underprivileged, and the discriminated against. He uses it to proclaim His word in preaching and teaching. In other words, God uses His Church as the body of Christ, doing in the world now what Christ did in his own time during the earthly dimension of his existence.

In the liturgy, however, God acts in a special way. Through particular and special actions, called the sacraments, God acts in particular and special ways in the lives of His people. First, He acts in their lives in a way He does not act in the lives of those who cannot or do not receive the sacraments. Second, He produces effects in the lives of those who receive the sacraments that are not produced in the lives of those who do not. Thus, those who receive the sacraments have a special kind of relationship with God.

4.2 What Are the Sacraments?

Almost all Catholics take the sacraments for granted. They have a vague notion of what they are, think they know what the sacraments "do," and receive them when they think they should. Most Catholics, too, think that only Catholics have sacraments.

The fact is, all religions have sacraments. They just do not call them that. Christianity borrowed the word from the pre-Christian use of the Latin word *sacramentum,* meaning a pledge, a sign, or solemn oath. Because the pledge or oath was made in a temple or sacred place, it became something sacred or holy. Later, the word was used to mean the pledge of allegiance a new soldier made to his commander, to the emperor of Rome, and to the Roman gods.

It came into the Christian Church because it was used to designate the action, similar to the soldier's, by which a person became a Christian—Baptism. A Christian "recruit" renounced his former life and swore allegiance to Christ his new lord.

> The purpose of the sacraments is to santify [people], to build up the body of Christ, and finally, to give worship to God.
>
> Constitution on the Sacred Liturgy

Holy Sepulchre Church Doorway—Jerusalem

Those actions we have come to call the seven sacraments are signs of God's acting in a special way in the life of an individual Catholic. They have been variously called signs of Christ, signs of grace, or acts of Christ. They are known as encounters with God, celebrations of life, and participation in Jesus' worship of the Father. Joseph Martos, an authority on the history of the sacraments, calls them doors to the sacred. Others refer to them as God's instruments, God's channels of grace, or the Divine Mysteries. Whatever they may be called, however, they are special actions of Christ in his Church which are true signs of the sacred realities taking place in the individual.

For Catholics, these special actions of Christ are **Baptism, Confirmation,** the **Eucharist, the Sacrament of Reconciliation,** the **Anointing of the Sick, Holy Orders, and Matrimony.** For Catholics, each sacrament has its own purpose and special grace. Each has its own meaning and place in the life of each individual Catholic.

To properly understand the sacraments, it is necessary to view them from the standpoint of God's saving presence in the world. The sacraments are not isolated acts, either of God, of the Church, or of an individual. They are not God's "rewards" for our being "good." They are not little "gifts of God," or things we do to be close to God. *The whole sacramental process is a sanctifying process preparing us for total union with God in eternity.*

As we have said (and it demands repetition), God created people to share His life with them. This is the purpose of life. It is the reason for our existence. It is

Later, the word came to mean any sacred action, symbol, or ceremony like blessings, relics, other holy objects, or anything used as a sign of a sacred event or reality. (That is why we say that all religions have sacraments, even though they do not call them such.) Finally, the word sacrament was used to designate what became known as the seven sacraments only. Other sacred things or actions, like the sign of the cross, holy water, or visits to the Blessed Sacrament became known as "sacramentals," meaning "like a sacrament." They, too, are signs of sacred actions, of sacred realities, or of God's action.*

---

*Protestant Christians generally do not have seven sacraments. Most have only two, Baptism and the Lord's Supper, though some include other actions like marriage and confirmation.

the object of the whole range of dynamic forces at work in the universe. Everything that has happened from the first instant of creation to this moment in history is part of the determined plan of God to share His life with people. It may be difficult to see at times, and very difficult to understand at others, but there is a plan, an order, and a progression to creation. This plan, this order, and this progression lead to the fulfillment of the Divine Plan. There is a direct cause-and-effect relationship.

The progression of God's plan, like the development of His Self-revelation was gradual, consisting of very definite steps or stages. Step one was the act of creation itself. Step two was the evolutionary development of the universe to the point where it could sustain primitive life forms. Step three was the emergence and development of conscious life forms (animals). Step four was the development of self-conscious life forms (people). Step five was the formation of a people into the people of God in a direct covenant relationship in the desert. Step six was the coming of God into His creation in the person of Jesus. The whole process was pointing toward one thing: the sanctifying of creation. The presence of Jesus

made this sanctification a fact. The actions of Jesus made it a reality in the lives of individuals who encountered him.

In Jesus, people encountered God in Person. His actions were the actions of God. God was no longer far off, or "in the mind," or "in a building," or only in an assembly of His people. He was there in Person. He was no longer acting simply outside of His people as an agent. He was acting in them as a Divine Force or Energy.

When he was about to leave his disciples, Jesus established a means whereby he would "not leave them orphans." He would, as he said, "come back to you." (See John 14:18.) This means was his Church, his body in the world. It was the body through which he would act in the world. So, the saving presence of God in the world now, the sanctifying presence as we call it, is the Church.

It is in the acts of the Church, in the liturgy, then, that Catholics encounter Christ in the same way as those who lived with him encountered him: in his person. He is present in his Church and acts there, as he did formerly, through human acts and signs whereby people are

I will ask the Father and he will give you another Paraclete to be with you always... The Spirit of truth will remain with you and will be within you. (John 14: 16,17)

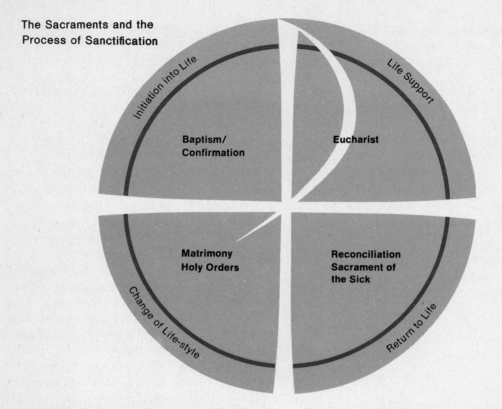

The Sacraments and the
Process of Sanctification

Initiation into Life

Life Support

**Baptism/
Confirmation**

Eucharist

**Matrimony
Holy Orders**

**Reconciliation
Sacrament of
the Sick**

Change of Life-style

Return to Life

sanctified. These human acts and signs are the sacraments.

But the sacraments, as we said, are not isolated acts, and they are not simply "helps," nor "grace" as an isolated object. They are encounters with the Person of Christ. This personal encounter, once begun in Baptism, is continuous, dynamic, and creative (unless totally destroyed by serious sin). It produces an ever-increasing holiness as a person matures in the sacramental life.

Once it is understood that the sacraments as a whole are part of the sanctifying process, it becomes easier to understand the unity of the sacramental system, and the role each sacrament plays in the process of sanctification. Viewed as a whole, the sacramental process is continuous and developmental.

Viewed individually, each sacrament plays a role in the process of sanctification. **(See the diagram above.)**

In the space below or on another sheet of paper, write three statements from your book which best say for you what a sacrament is.

In the diagram on page 110, what does the symbol ⱷ mean?

Be sure that you can recite the steps in the Divine Plan to bring people to a full share in the Divine Life. What is the role of the sacraments in this plan?

When does the special kind of relationship Catholics believe they have with God begin? When does it end? Explain.

Why the Special Relationship Occurs

The special relationship with God which Catholics believe they have through the sacraments occurs because of the five factors which are part of each sacrament. These five make each sacrament what it is and make each a part of the total sanctifying process.

The first is that God's specific action, signified by the actual reception of the sacrament and by the symbols and rites connected with each, occurs at a time which is in keeping with the period of maturity in a person's life. Baptism, for example, initiates a person into the Christian life. The Sacrament of Matrimony marks the beginning of a new family relationship. The Sacrament of the Sick offers comfort at the time when a sick person most needs it. Everything that is said and done in each sacrament points to and brings out its significance and purpose.

The second factor is that each sacrament contains the *moment* of God's sacramental action (it does occur at a particular time) and the *action* of God signified by the sacrament. (Christ does become present in the Eucharist when the words of consecration are said by the priest.)

The third factor is that the special action of God in a sacrament is continuous. It operates in a person's life from the time he or she participates in the sacrament. The rite or ceremony does not constitute the whole of the sacrament; it only initiates the action of God in the sacrament. The wedding ceremony, for example, is not the whole of the sacrament. Living together in the married life is the sacrament. The baptismal ceremony is not the whole of the sacrament. Living the Christian life is.

Like the action of Christ in his dealings with people, the rite or ceremony is only one step in the entire process of a sacrament.* The absolution by the priest, for example, while constituting an absolutely necessary ingredient of the Sacrament of Reconciliation, is still only one step in the entire process of reconciliation. The first step, initiated by God's grace, is the sinner's recognition of his or her sinful action or sinful state. The second step is sorrow for sin, and the third is the confession of sin to a designated minister of the sacrament. The fourth is the absolution by the priest, acting as Christ for the penitent. The fifth step is the turning away from sin or the

habit of sin and the living of the Christian life in grace. All of these make up the sacrament. God's *special* grace in the Sacrament of Reconciliation acts in the life of the person from the moment of the priest's action.

The fourth factor inherent in each sacrament that makes it what it is and makes it a part of the total sanctification process, is that God initiates the action to holiness. In each sacrament, it is God who goes in search of His people. It is God who calls. It is God who offers His help. It is God who selects the person and the time for His particular grace. It is the person who accepts—or rejects—the grace of the sacrament. It is the person who accepts—or rejects—the offer to grow spiritually and to develop his or her relationship with God, which is the very essence of holiness.

Finally, it should be remembered, that the sacraments are not for an individual alone. All the sacraments in general, and each in particular, have a social dimension that affects the world. When a person accepts God's grace in the sacraments, he not only becomes holier himself; the world becomes holier. Through Baptism, for example, the body of Christ is built up and more people

---

*In curing the paralyzed man, for example, Jesus recognized the intention of the people who brought him and the man's intention; only then did he act in the man's favor. " 'Get up,' Jesus said to him. 'Take your bedding with you and go home.' Immediately the man got up and went home, praising God." (Luke 5:17–25) All of Christ's miracles affecting people follow the same pattern. See, for example, the Cana miracle (John 2), the bringing back to life of the young girl (Mark 5), and the incident involving the centurion's servant (Matthew 8).

The sacraments are deliberately and specifically designed to open to us the realm of sacred reality.

Joseph Martos

experience God's particular saving actions in their lives. Through the Sacrament of Reconciliation, the social effects of sin are lessened. Through Ordination, the ministry is extended and more people hear the word of God proclaimed. Through them all, God's saving presence is experienced in the world and the world is better for it.

Name and explain each of the factors above by illustrating with a single sacrament not mentioned in your book. For example, the "moment of God's sacramental action" in . . . is. . . .

Read carefully the last two sentences of the opening quotation. Spend a few moments thinking about them, then be prepared to say what they mean to you.

In what sense is it true to say that:

The universe is the sign of God the Creator,

People are the sign of God the Lover,

Christ is the sign of God the Savior,

The Church is the sign of Christ to the world,

The Sacraments are the signs of the Church that Christ lives and acts in his people?

Why Are There Seven Sacraments?

In the Catholic Church there are seven sacraments because, over the course of the centuries, the Church recognized that seven sacramental actions were geared to the seven basic spiritual needs of individuals as they moved through life. Other sacramental actions seemed not as important and did not produce the same effects. These seven became known as "the sacraments" and other sacramental actions remained "sacramentals."

Each sacrament has its own matter (material used), form (words said), and rituals (actions), and each has its own symbolization. That is, each action, word, and material represents, points to, or signifies the reality of God's action in the sacrament.

The bread and wine, for example, in the Eucharist not only look and taste like food, they are the spiritual food of the one receiving them. They become the spiritual food because, after the Consecration in the Mass, they are the body and blood of Christ, the spiritual nourishment of Christians.

The seven basic spiritual needs and the sacraments that meet those needs are:

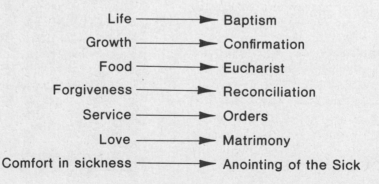

Life ——————▶ Baptism

Growth ——————▶ Confirmation

Food ——————▶ Eucharist

Forgiveness ——————▶ Reconciliation

Service ——————▶ Orders

Love ——————▶ Matrimony

Comfort in sickness ——————▶ Anointing of the Sick

Some sacraments are received only once; some are received often. The frequency is determined by what the sacrament is and does. Baptism, Confirmation, and Orders, for example, are received only once. It is evident that a person can be initiated into the Christian community only once—that is, he can become a Christian only once. Even if he renounces his faith forever or for a short time, he has been incorporated into the body of Christ and cannot be "unincorporated." After Baptism, a person has a special and permanent relationship with God which God will not renounce.

It is the same with Confirmation and Orders. A person is sealed with the Spirit of Christ in Confirmation. The Holy Spirit lives and acts in that person forever. A person can be ordained only once because the reality of ordination cannot be lost.

The other sacraments, Eucharist, Reconciliation, Anointing of the Sick, and Matrimony can be received whenever the effect they cause is needed.

Through the sacraments, as we have just seen, a person enjoys a special kind of relationship with God. This special relationship is begun in Baptism—the first, or initial, sacrament of the Church. It is sealed, or confirmed, in the second sacrament received by an individual in the Catholic Church, Confirmation.

4.3 Beginning the Special Relationship in Baptism

Baptism is the first sacrament of the Christian Church because through it a person becomes a Christian. It is often called "a sacrament of initiation" because through it people are initiated into the Christian community.

Baptism is also often called a sign of belonging and a sign of transformation. It is called a sacrament of belonging because through it a person "belongs" to Christ, and "belongs" to a faith community. It is called a sacrament of transformation because by it a person is transformed from a person who has only natural life to one who has a "super" natural life. Each person has within himself or herself, in a special way, the life of God. The newly baptized person is transformed from a person who had a general relationship with God to one who has a special relationship with Him.

Just as God created people in His image (Genesis 1:27), so does Jesus make people in his own image through the sacraments. He begins this process in Baptism by elevating human nature and enabling people to live in a new dimension of existence—the divine dimension—by giving them his own divine life.

This new life, or "super" natural life as we have called it, given in Baptism, is the life intended for people by God when He created them. It is the life toward which the dynamic forces implanted in creation by God are moving the human race. It is a dimension of life beyond, or above, the life received at conception. That is why we call it "super" natural. It is a gift of God, given to those whom He selects to be His Christs to the world.

Christians believe this about Baptism because of what Jesus taught. His teaching about this supernatural life is, perhaps, best summarized in the following account of a conversation he had with an educated Jew:

There was a man named Nicodemus, a leader of the Jews, who belonged to the party of the Pharisees.

One night he came to Jesus and said to him: "We know, Rabbi, that you are a teacher sent by God. No one could do the mighty works you are doing unless God were with him." Jesus answered, "I tell you the truth: no one can see the Kingdom of God unless he is born again." "How can a grown man be born again?" Nicodemus asked. "He certainly cannot enter his mother's womb and be born a second time!" "I tell you the

truth," replied Jesus, "that no one can enter the Kingdom of God unless he is born of water and the Spirit. Flesh gives birth to flesh, and Spirit gives birth to spirit. Do not be surprised because I tell you, 'You must all be born again.' The wind blows wherever it wishes; you hear the sound it makes, but you do not know where it comes from or where it is going. It is the same way with everyone who is born of the Spirit."

"How can this be?" asked Nicodemus. Jesus answered: "You are a great teacher of Israel, and you don't know this? I tell you the truth: we speak of what we know, and tell what we have seen—yet none of you is willing to accept our message. You do not believe me when I tell you about the things of this world; how will you ever believe me, then, when I tell you about the things of heaven? And no one has ever gone up to heaven except the Son of Man, who came down from heaven."

As Moses lifted up the bronze snake on a pole in the desert, in the same way the Son of Man must be lifted up, so that everyone who believes in him may have eternal life. For God loved the world so much that he gave his only Son, so that everyone who believes in him may not die but have eternal life. For God did not send his Son into the world to be its Judge, but to be its Savior.

(John 3:1–17)

4.4 Why Should a Person Be Baptized?

In addition to transforming a person and enabling him or her to begin a new relationship with God, Baptism brings with it certain privileges which also are compelling reasons for Baptism.

First, Baptism marks our birth as Christians. Through it we become other Christs. (For many centuries, Baptism was administered in many places by immersing a person in water. This was to symbolize both a person's death to his former life and his birth as a Christian. Many times the baptismal font was shaped like a tomb to further this death-and-rebirth symbol. Many times, too, the baptismal font was called "the womb of the Church" because from it were born Christians.) This "second" birth (into God's family) made a person a member of the body of Christ—a real part of the body by which Christ shows himself to the world. "It was in one Spirit that all of us . . . were baptized into one body," says St. Paul. "You, then, are the body of Christ. Every one of you is a member of it." (1 Corinthians 12:13, 27)

The second privilege is that a person becomes the dwelling-place of the Holy Trinity because every baptized person becomes as it were a temple in which God lives. "Are you not aware that you are the temple of God and that the Spirit of God dwells in you? . . . the temple of God is holy, and you are that temple." (1 Corinthians 3:16–17)

Sixth, Baptism prepares a person for the Christian life and enables him to live as a Christian if he cooperates with the grace of the sacrament.

Seventh, Baptism readies a person for sharing God's life in a fuller, deeper way when he assumes his own risen life after earthly death.

It is for these reasons, and others, of course, that a person should be baptized and should try to live the Christian life as perfectly as he or she possibly can, given the circumstances of the individual's life. It is for these reasons, too, that parents should have their children baptized as soon as is reasonably possible. After all, an infant can receive God's grace and begin a new life and a new relationship with God as well as a teenager or an adult can!

It ought to be noted that the effects of Baptism are not felt physically or exteriorly. (There is, however, often a deep emotional and psychological effect in adults.) There is no automatic change in a person's makeup or character. The change is within. It brings a person the grace of God—the energy, force, and desire to live the Christian life, and the continued grace to do so.

Baptism does not, either, insure against a person's committing sin or failing in his or her baptismal promises. If it did, it would violate a person's freedom—and God never does that. He offers His help; He does not force.

Third, Baptism confers on the person baptized the grace of mission. He or she is called to join in Christ's work of establishing the kingdom of God on earth, and is given God's special help for this mission.

Fourth, Baptism grants the privilege of participating in the Eucharistic celebration of God's saving acts in Christ and of receiving the body of Christ.

Fifth, Baptism admits a person to the other sacraments through which he receives God's special help in the most important developments in his life.

The Matter and Form
in Baptism

The Church baptizes because Jesus directed it to do so.

> "Full authority has been given to me both in heaven and on earth," said Jesus just before he ascended into heaven. "Go, therefore, and make disciples of all the nations. Baptize them in the name of the Father, and of the Son, and of the Holy Spirit. Teach them to carry out everything I have commanded you. And know that I am with you always, until the end of the world!" (Matthew 28: 18–20)

To baptize, the Church uses water (the matter) to symbolize the cleansing and life-giving properties of Baptism. It uses the words given in the Gospel of Matthew (the form). It directs the baptizer to pour water on the head of the person to be baptized (or to immerse in water) while saying the words (the ritual). Other things may be done or added if they are in good taste and in keeping with the nature of the sacrament, but the water, the words, and the action are necessary for the baptism to be valid, or proper.

The ordinary minister of Baptism in the Catholic Church is a priest. Anyone may baptize, however, and any baptism that is performed properly is a valid sacrament and brings with it the effects and privileges of Baptism. It should be noted that a person is never rebaptized, as we said. However, a person may be baptized *conditionally* if there is any doubt about a previous baptism.

In most instances, especially in formal baptisms, the baptized has what are called "sponsors." This practice arose in the early Church when people were converted from paganism. Their preparation for Baptism took place over a long period of time. During that time they were instructed and "practiced" being Christians. At the time of their baptism, they had to have people stand up for them and testify that while they were "catechumens" they did, indeed, live good lives. The person who so testified was called a "sponsor."

Nowadays, sponsors are largely ceremonial in adult baptisms. In infant baptisms, sponsors respond to the questions asked in place of the infant and stand ready to raise the child as a Christian if anything should happen to the parents.

When the Church baptizes a child, that action concerns me, for that child is thereby connected to that which is my head too, and ingrafted into that body whereof I am a member.

John Donne

A practice that is more and more falling into disuse in modern times is the naming of children after saints. For many years, Mary was the most popular name for girls and John for boys. The Church does not advise one way or another about names. All it asks is that the parents consider the adolescent feelings of the child being named so that, later in life, the child will not feel embarrassed or ashamed.

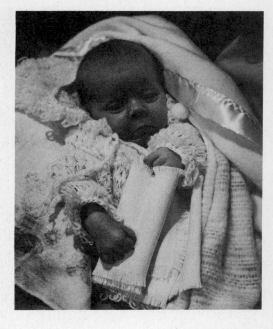

Below is a short-form baptismal rite. Read it carefully, then, on a sheet of paper, answer the questions which follow.

Celebrating New Life in the Church*

1. RECEPTION OF THE CHILD

The celebrating priest, vested, greets the parents who have brought the child to be baptized.

PRIEST: What do you ask of God's Church for this child?

PARENTS: *Baptism.*

PRIEST: The Christian community welcomes you with great joy. In its name I claim you for Christ our Savior by the sign of the cross.

*The material given here contains only the principal parts of the rite of baptism. The complete rite is given on page 123.

2. CELEBRATION OF GOD'S WORD AND PRAYER

A gospel passage is read, after which the priest explains the mystery of baptism.

PRIEST: By the mystery of your death and resurrection, Lord, bathe this child in light, give him [her] the new life of baptism and welcome him [her] into your holy Church.

PRIEST: Almighty and everliving God, we pray for this child. Set him [her] free from sin, make him [her] a temple of your glory, and send your Holy Spirit to dwell with him [her]. We ask this through Christ our Lord.

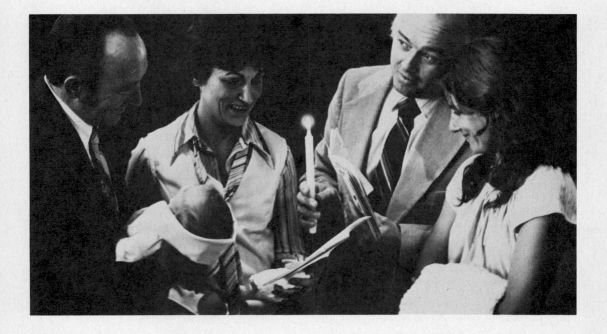

3. CELEBRATION OF THE SACRAMENT

PRIEST: My dear friends, God uses the sacrament of water to give His divine life to those who believe in Him. Let us turn to Him and ask Him to pour his gift of life from this font on this child He has chosen.

PRIEST: I baptize you in the name of the Father, and of the Son, and of the Holy Spirit.

PRIEST: God the Father of our Lord Jesus Christ has freed you from sin, given you a new birth by water and the Holy Spirit, and welcomed you into His holy people. He now anoints you with the chrism of salvation. As Christ was anointed Priest, Prophet, and King, so may you live always as a member of his body, sharing everlasting life.

4. CONCLUSION TO THE RITE OF BAPTISM

PRIEST: This child has been reborn in baptism. He [she] is now called the child of God, for so indeed he [she] is. In confirmation he [she] will receive the fullness of God's Spirit. In holy communion he [she] will share the banquet of Christ's sacrifice, calling God his [her] Father in the midst of the Church. In the name of this child, in the Spirit of our common sonship, let us pray together in the words our Lord has given us.

The celebrant first blesses the mother, who holds the child in her arms, then the father, and lastly the entire assembly.

PRIEST: By God's gift, through water and the Holy Spirit, we are reborn to everlasting life. In His Goodness, may He continue to pour out His blessings upon these sons and daughters of His. May He make them always, wherever they may be, faithful members of His holy people. May He send His peace upon all who are gathered here, in Christ Jesus our Lord.

What is the "moment" of the sacrament?

What matter is used? What is the form used?

What rituals does the priest follow?

Name three things which are used as symbols and tell what they symbolize.

What other sacraments are mentioned? Why are they mentioned?

What things are added to the essentials of Baptism?

What privileges of Baptism are mentioned?

In whose name is the baptism conferred? How do you know?

In the quotation from the Gospel according to John 3:14, the phrase "bronze snake" is used. It comes from the Old Testament, Numbers 21:4-9. Look up the reference and be prepared to tell why you think Jesus used the expression.

Explain why the life conferred in Baptism is called "super" natural life. According to your book, for what life do the sacraments, especially Baptism, prepare us?

Why does it say that that is the life we are preparing for?

Name four of the privileges that accompany Baptism.

Why does the Church baptize?

Baptism Is a Celebration

Because of the belonging and transforming aspect of Baptism, it is *the* sacrament of the Church. It transforms a person and enables him or her to belong to Christ's Body, the Church. Through it, the Body of Christ becomes a reality in each era, and Christ lives and acts as he lived and acted during his earthly life.

Baptism causes the Divine Life to blossom in the one being baptized and brings about a special relationship with God. It carries with it special privileges and begins the process which will bring a person to a full share in the Divine Life for all eternity.

It is because of these realities that Baptism is *celebrated* in the Catholic Church. It is an occasion of joy not only for the individual but for the whole Church. For that reason it is, ideally, celebrated during Sunday Mass when the parish family, representing the whole Church, is gathered to worship God. Even if it cannot be celebrated during Mass, it is still a celebration. It is a celebration of the wonderful works of God in the world.

As we said earlier, a sacrament is a sign of God's acting in a special and particular way in the life of an individual and in the life of the Church. We said that receiving a sacrament is part of the Divine process for bringing people to holiness.

We have also said that every sacrament signifies, points to, and brings about, the sacred reality of which it is a visible expression. The "Rite for the Baptism of One Child" during Mass which follows is a good example of the sign, symbol, ritual, and reality aspects of a sacrament.

Rite of Baptism for One Child (During Mass)

1. INTRODUCTORY RITE: RECEPTION OF THE CHILD

(This Introductory Rite replaces the ordinary rite used at the beginning of Mass.)

It is the role of the father and mother, accompanied by the godparents, to present the child to the Church for baptism.

The people may sing a psalm or hymn suitable for the occasion. Meanwhile the celebrating priest or deacon, vested in alb or surplice, with a stole (with or without a cope) of festive color, and accompanied by the ministers, goes to the entrance of the church or to that part of the church where the parents and godparents are waiting with the child.

The celebrant greets all present, and especially the parents and godparents, reminding them briefly of the joy with which the parents welcomed this child as a gift from God, the source of life, who now wishes to bestow his own life on this little one.

First the celebrant questions the parents:

CELEBRANT: What name do you give your child? [or: have you given?]

PARENTS: *N.*

CELEBRANT: What do you ask of God's Church for N.?

PARENTS: *Baptism.*

The celebrant may choose other words for this dialogue.

The first reply may be given by someone other than the parents if local custom give him the right to name the child.

In the second response the parents may use other words, such as "faith" or "the grace of Christ" or "entrance into the Church" or "eternal life."

The celebrant speaks to the parents in these or similar words:

CELEBRANT: You have asked to have your child baptized. In doing so you are accepting the

responsibility of training him [her] in the practice of the faith. It will be your duty to bring him [her] up to keep God's commandments as Christ taught us, by loving God and our neighbor. Do you clearly understand what you are undertaking?

PARENTS: *We do.*

Then the celebrant turns to the godparents and addresses them in these or similar words:

CELEBRANT: Are you ready to help the parents of this child in their duty as Christian parents?

GODPARENTS: *We are.*

The celebrant continues:

CELEBRANT: N., the Christian community welcomes you with great joy. In its name I claim you for Christ our Savior by the sign of his cross. I now trace the cross on your forehead, and invite your parents [and godparents] to do the same.

He signs the child on the forehead, in silence. Then he invites the parents and (if it seems appropriate) the godparents to do the same.

The celebrant invites the parents, godparents, and the others to take part in the liturgy of the word.

2. CELEBRATION OF GOD'S WORD

Scriptural Readings and Homily

One or even two gospel passages are read, during which all may sit if convenient.

PRIEST: A reading from the holy gospel according to Matthew:
Jesus came forward and addressed the eleven disciples in these words: "Full authority has been given to me both in heaven and on earth; go, therefore, and make disciples of all the nations. Baptize them in the name 'of the Father and of the Son, and of the Holy Spirit.' Teach them to carry out everything I have commanded you. And know that I am with you always, until the end of the world!"

Matthew 28:18–20

Other readings, together with responsorial psalms and verses before the gospel, may be selected as long as they are appropriate.

After the reading, the celebrant gives a short homily, explaining to those present the significance of what has been read. His purpose will be to lead them to a deeper understanding of the mystery of baptism and to encourage the parents and godparents to a ready acceptance of the responsibilities which arise from the sacrament.

After the homily, or in the course of or after the litany, it is desirable to have a period of silence while all pray at the invitation of the celebrant. Then the prayer of the faithful is said.

CELEBRANT: My dear brothers and sisters,* let us ask our Lord Jesus Christ to look lovingly on this child who is to be baptized, on his [her] parents and godparents, and on all the baptized.

LEADER: By the mystery of your death and resurrection, bathe this child in light, give him [her] the new life of baptism and welcome him [her] into your holy Church.

PEOPLE: *Lord, hear our prayer.*

LEADER: Through baptism and confirmation, make him [her] your faithful follower and a witness to your gospel.

PEOPLE: *Lord, hear our prayer.*

LEADER: Lead him [her] by a holy life to the joys of God's kingdom.

PEOPLE: *Lord, hear our prayer.*

LEADER: Make the lives of his [her] parents and godparents examples of faith to inspire this child.

PEOPLE: *Lord, hear our prayer.*

LEADER: Keep his [her] family always in your love.

PEOPLE: *Lord, hear our prayer.*

LEADER: Renew the grace of our baptism in each one of us.

PEOPLE: *Lord, hear our prayer.*

The celebrant next invites all present to invoke the saints.

Holy Mary, Mother of God, *pray for us.*

Saint John the Baptist, *pray for us.*

Saint Joseph, *pray for us.*

Saint Peter and Saint Paul, *pray for us.*

The names of other saints may be added, especially the patrons of the child to be baptized, and of the church or locality. The litany concludes:

All you saints of God, *pray for us.*

---

*At the discretion of the priest, other words which seem more suitable under the circumstances, such as "friends, dearly beloved, brethren," may be used. This also applies to parallel instances in the liturgy.

Prayer of Exorcism and Anointing before Baptism

After the invocation, the celebrant says:

CELEBRANT: Almighty and
ever-living God, you sent your
only Son into the world to cast
out the power of Satan, spirit of evil,
to rescue man from the kingdom of darkness,
and bring him into the splendor of your
    kingdom of light.
We pray for this child:
set him [her] free from original sin,
make him [her] a temple of your glory,
and send your Holy Spirit to dwell with him
    [her].
[We ask this] through Christ our Lord.

PEOPLE: *Amen.*

The celebrant continues:

We anoint you with the oil of salvation in
the name of Christ our Savior; may he
strengthen you with his power, who lives and
reigns for ever and ever.

PEOPLE: *Amen.*

He anoints the child on the breast with the
oil of catechumens.

The anointing before baptism may be
omitted if the celebrant judges the omission to
be pastorally necessary or desirable. In that case
he says:

May you have strength in the power of
Christ our Savior, who lives and reigns for ever
and ever.

PEOPLE: *Amen.*

And immediately he lays his hand on the
child in silence.

Then they go to the baptistry, or to the
sanctuary when baptism is celebrated there on
occasion.

3. CELEBRATION OF THE SACRAMENT

When they come to the font, the celebrant
briefly reminds the congregation of the
wonderful work of God whose plan it is to
sanctify man, body and soul, through water. He

125

may use these or similar words:

My dear brothers and sisters, we now ask God to give this child new life in abundance through water and the Holy Spirit.

or: My dear brothers and sisters, God uses the sacrament of water to give his divine life to those who believe in him. Let us turn to him, and ask him to pour his gift of life from this font on this child he has chosen.

Blessing and Invocation of God over Baptismal Water

Then, turning to the font, he says the following blessing:

CELEBRANT: Father, you give us grace through sacramental signs, which tell us of the wonders of your unseen power.

In baptism we use your gift of water, which you have made a rich symbol of the grace you give us in this sacrament.

At the very dawn of creation your Spirit breathed on the waters, making them the well-spring of all holiness.

The waters of the great flood you made a sign of the waters of baptism, that make an end of sin and a new beginning of goodness.

Through the waters of the Red Sea you led Israel out of slavery, to be an image of God's holy people, set free from sin by baptism.

In the waters of the Jordan your Son was baptized by John and anointed with the Spirit.

Your Son willed that water and blood should flow from his side as he hung upon the cross.

After his resurrection he told his disciples: "Go out and teach all nations, baptizing them in the name of the Father, and of the Son, and of the Holy Spirit."

Father, look now with love upon your Church, and unseal for her the fountain of baptism.

By the power of the spirit give to the water of this font the grace of your Son.

You created man in your own likeness:
cleanse him from sin in a new birth to innocence
by water and the Spirit.

The celebrant touches the water with his
right hand and continues:

We ask you, Father, with your Son to send
the Holy Spirit upon the water of this font.
May all who are buried with Christ in the death
of baptism rise also with him to newness of life.
[We ask this] through Christ our Lord.

PEOPLE: *Amen.*

CELEBRANT: Dear parents and godparents: You
have come here to present this child for
baptism. By water and the Holy Spirit he [she]
is to receive the gift of new life from God, who
is love.

On your part, you must make it your
constant care to bring him [her] up in the
practice of the faith. See that the divine life
which God gives him [her] is kept safe from the
poison of sin, to grow always stronger in his
[her] heart.

If your faith makes you ready to accept this
responsibility, renew now the vows of your own
baptism. Reject sin; profess your faith in Christ
Jesus. This is the faith of the Church. This is
the faith in which this child is about to be
baptized.

The celebrant questions the parents and
godparents.

CELEBRANT: Do you reject sin, so as to live in
the freedom of God's children?

PARENTS AND GODPARENTS: *I do.*

Renunciation of Sin and Profession of Faith

The celebrant speaks to the parents and
godparents in these words:

CELEBRANT: Do you reject the glamor of evil,
and refuse to be mastered by sin?

PARENTS AND GODPARENTS: *I do.*

CELEBRANT: Do you reject Satan, father of sin
and prince of darkness?

PARENTS AND GODPARENTS: *I do.*

Next the celebrant asks for the threefold
profession of faith from the parents and
godparents:

CELEBRANT: Do you believe in God, the Father
almighty, creator of heaven and earth?

PARENTS AND GODPARENTS: *I do.*

CELEBRANT: Do you believe in Jesus Christ, his
only Son, our Lord, who was born of the Virgin
Mary, was crucified, died, and was buried, rose
from the dead, and is now seated at the right
hand of the Father?

PARENTS AND GODPARENTS: *I do.*

CELEBRANT: Do you believe in the Holy Spirit,
the holy catholic Church, the communion of
saints, the forgiveness of sins, the resurrection of
the body, and life everlasting?

PARENTS AND GODPARENTS: *I do.*

The celebrant and the congregation give their
assent to this profession of faith:

CELEBRANT: This is our faith. This is the faith
of the Church. We are proud to profess it, in
Christ Jesus our Lord.

ALL: *Amen.*

Baptism

The celebrant invites the family to the font
and questions the parents and godparents:

CELEBRANT: Is it your will that N. should be
baptized in the faith of the Church, which we
have all professed with you?

PARENTS AND GODPARENTS: *It is.*

He baptizes the child, saying:

CELEBRANT: N., I baptize you in the name of
the Father,

He immerses the child or pours water upon
it.

CELEBRANT: and of the Son,

He immerses the child or pours water upon
it a second time.

CELEBRANT: and of the Holy Spirit.

He immerses the child or pours water upon
it a third time.

After the child is baptized, it is appropriate for the people to sing a short acclamation:

This is the fountain of life,
water made holy by the suffering of Christ,
washing all the world.
You who are washed in this water
have hope of heaven's kingdom.

Anointing with Chrism

CELEBRANT: God the Father of our Lord Jesus Christ has freed you from sin, given you a new birth by water and the Holy Spirit, and welcomed you into his holy people. He now anoints you with the chrism of salvation. As Christ was anointed Priest, Prophet, and King, so may you live always as a member of his body, sharing everlasting life.

PEOPLE: *Amen.*

Then the celebrant anoints the child on the crown of the head with the sacred chrism, in silence.

Clothing with the White Garment

CELEBRANT: N., you have become a new creation, and have clothed yourself in Christ. See in this white garment the outward sign of your Christian dignity. With your family and friends to help you by word and example, bring that dignity unstained into the everlasting life of heaven.

PEOPLE: *Amen.*

The white garment is put on the child. A different color is not permitted unless demanded by local custom. It is desirable that the family provide the garment.

Lighted Candle

The celebrant takes the Easter candle.

CELEBRANT: Receive the light of Christ.

Someone from the family (such as the father or godfather) lights the child's candle from the Easter candle.

CELEBRANT: Parents and godparents, this light is entrusted to you to be kept burning brightly. This child of yours has been enlightened by Christ. He [she] is to walk always as a child of the light. May he [she] keep the flame of faith alive in his [her] heart. When the Lord comes, may he [she] go out to meet him with all the saints in the heavenly kingdom.

Ephphetha or Prayer over Ears and Mouth

The rite of *Ephphetha* may be performed at the discretion of the celebrant. He touches the ears and mouth of the child with his thumb, saying:

CELEBRANT: The Lord Jesus made the deaf hear and the dumb speak. May he soon touch your ears to receive his word, and your mouth to proclaim his faith, to the praise and glory of God the Father.

PEOPLE: *Amen.*

4. CONCLUSION OF THE RITE

Next, there is a procession to the altar, unless the baptism was performed in the sanctuary. The lighted candle is carried for the child.

A baptismal song is appropriate at this time, e.g.:

You have put on Christ,
in him you have been baptized.
Alleluia, alleluia.

Lord's Prayer

The celebrant stands in front of the altar and addresses the parents, godparents, and the whole assembly in these or similar words.

CELEBRANT: Dearly beloved, this child has been reborn in baptism. He [she] is now called the child of God, for so indeed he [she] is. In confirmation he [she] will receive the fullness of God's Spirit. In holy communion he [she] will share the banquet of Christ's sacrifice, calling God his [her] Father in the midst of the Church. In the name of this child, in the Spirit of our common sonship, let us pray together in the words our Lord has given us:

All present join the celebration in singing or saying:

PEOPLE:
Our Father,
who art in heaven,
hallowed be thy name;
thy kingdom come;
thy will be done on earth as it is in heaven.

Give us this day our daily bread;
and forgive us our trespasses
as we forgive those who trespass against us;
and lead us not into temptation,
but deliver us from evil.

Blessing

The celebrant first blesses the mother, who holds the child in her arms, then the father, and lastly the entire assembly:

CELEBRANT: God the Father, through his Son, the Virgin Mary's child, has brought joy to all Christian mothers, as they see the hope of eternal life shine on their children. May he bless the mother of this child. She now thanks God for the gift of her child. May she be one with him in thanking him for ever in heaven in Christ Jesus our Lord.

PEOPLE: *Amen.*

CELEBRANT: God is the giver of all life, human and divine. May he bless the father of this child. He and his wife will be the first teachers of their child in the ways of faith. May they be also the best of teachers, bearing witness to the faith by what they say and do, in Christ Jesus our Lord.

PEOPLE: *Amen.*

CELEBRANT: By God's gift, through water and the Holy Spirit, we are reborn to everlasting life. In his goodness, may he continue to pour out his blessings upon these sons and daughters of his. May he make them always, wherever they may be, faithful members of his holy people. May he send his peace upon all who are gathered here, in Christ Jesus our Lord.

PEOPLE: *Amen.*

CELEBRANT: May almighty God, the Father, and the Son, and the Holy Spirit, bless you.

PEOPLE: *Amen.*

(After the blessings, all return to their places and Mass continues at the "Offertory.")

4.5 Sealing the Special Relationship through Confirmation

One of the most startling disclosures in the New Testament is the revelation of the existence of a Third Person in God. There are nearly 100 references in the New Testament speaking of the Holy Spirit, most of which speak of Him in active terms. His role in creation is to sanctify—to complete creation by bringing it to its fulfillment.

You are already familiar with the promise of Jesus to send his Spirit to his Apostles (John 16:7) and with the transforming action of the Holy Spirit at Pentecost described in Acts 2. What you may not be familiar with is that the Holy Spirit is given to every Christian as a Gift of the Father (John 14:16, 17). **This is the essence of the Sacrament of Confirmation.**

> I will ask the Father and he will give you another Paraclete*—to be with you always: the Spirit of truth, whom the world cannot accept, since it neither sees him nor recognizes him; but you must recognize him because he remains with you and will be within you. (John 14:16, 17)

The Holy Spirit is given to Christians to transform them from passive believers in Jesus to active participators in continuing God's creation. Through them, creation is to be transformed. This is the mission of the Holy Spirit in the world.

Confirmation, like Baptism, is an initiation sacrament in the Catholic Church. When people are baptized as adults, they ordinarily receive Confirmation immediately, either from a bishop present, or from a priest designated by the bishop. When Baptism is received by infants and children (or in emergency by adults), Confirmation is conferred at a later date. Hence, it is, really, an initiation sacrament.

Catholics believe that the Sacrament of Confirmation completes the reality of Baptism and is a sign of the conferring of the Holy Spirit because both are revealed in the New Testament. In describing the work of St. Paul in the first days of the Church, the Acts of the Apostles says:

> While Apollos was in Corinth, Paul traveled through the interior of the province and arrived in Ephesus. There he found some disciples, and asked them, "Did you receive the Holy Spirit when you believed?" "We have not even heard that there is a Holy Spirit," they answered. "Well, then, what kind of baptism did you receive?" Paul asked. "The baptism of John," they answered.* Paul said: "The baptism of John was for

---

*Paraclete means advocate, pleader of a cause, or one who comes to aid. Jesus says "another paraclete" because he is the "first paraclete."

*This was the baptism by John the Baptist described in Matthew 3:1–17. It was this baptism that Jesus received as a sign of the beginning of his mission.

130

those who turned from their sins; and he told the people of Israel that they should believe in the one who was coming after him—that is, in Jesus." When they heard this, they were baptized in the name of the Lord Jesus. Paul placed his hands on them, and the Holy Spirit came upon them. . . .   (Acts 19:1–6)

The Matter and Form of the Sacrament

The quotation above from the Acts reveals two important things. The first is that the action conferring the Holy Spirit is separate from the action of Baptism. The second is that the Spirit comes as a seal, or completion, of the sacrament of Baptism.

Thus, Confirmation is a sign of the seal of the Holy Spirit. For those who were baptized as infants or children, Confirmation is a sign that they personally accept the call of Christ that was accepted for them earlier. It is, also, a sign that a person accepts the duties and responsibilities of being an adult Christian.

Confirmation is an "active" sacrament. That is, for those who permit its effects to take hold of them, it releases the spiritual energies received through Baptism, and begins the maturing of the Gifts of the Holy Spirit.*

---

*The Gifts of the Holy Spirit are the spiritual gifts of wisdom, understanding, counsel, fortitude, knowledge, piety, and awe. They are gifts which enable a person to develop his or her spiritual life.

In Roman Catholic churches the Sacrament of Confirmation is ordinarily conferred by the bishop. The sacrament is received when the bishop, or designated minister, while making the sign of the cross with blessed oil on the forehead of the one being confirmed says: "N., receive the seal of the Holy Spirit, the Gift of the Father."

Through these words and actions, the "moment" of Confirmation takes place, the Holy Spirit is given by the Father, and the grace of giving witness is conferred. In this manner, Confirmation is a sign to the person and to the Church that the person and the Church are called to continue the work of Christ on earth.

Confirmation fittingly takes place in the Mass to show its fundamental relationship and connection with Baptism and the Eucharist and to stress its role as a sacrament of initiation. The person becomes a Christian through Baptism, receives its fullness in the Gift of the Spirit, and joins the Christian community in its formal praise of the Father and in its reception of the body and blood of Christ.

On the next page is a sample of the ritual used in the Sacrament of Confirmation. Study it carefully. On a separate sheet of paper, answer the questions that follow it.

Pentecost by a Westphalian Master, c. 1380

Rite of Confirmation
Outside Mass

1. ENTRANCE RITE

When the candidates, their sponsors and parents, and the whole assembly of the faithful have gathered, the bishop goes to the sanctuary with the priests who assist him, one or more deacons, and the ministers. Meanwhile all may sing a psalm or appropriate song.

The bishop makes the required reverence to the altar with the ministers and greets the people:

BISHOP: Peace be with you.

PEOPLE: *And also with you.*

Opening Prayer

Let us pray.

All pray in silence for a few moments. Then the bishop or one of the priests continues:
God of power and mercy, send your Holy Spirit to live in our hearts and make us temples of his glory.

Or:
Lord, fulfill your promise:
send your Holy Spirit
to make us witnesses before the world
to the Good News
proclaimed by Jesus Christ, our Lord.

Or:
Lord, send us your Holy Spirit
to help us walk in unity of faith
and grow in the strength of his love
to the full stature of Christ.

Or:
Lord, fulfill the promise
given by your Son
and send the Holy Spirit
to enlighten our minds
and lead us to all truth.

[We ask this] through Christ our Lord.

PEOPLE: *Amen.*

2. CELEBRATION OF THE WORD OF GOD

The celebration of the word of God follows. At least one of the readings suggested for the Mass of confirmation is read.

If two or three readings are chosen, the traditional order is followed; that is, the Old Testament, the Apostle, and the Gospel. After the first and second reading there should be a psalm or song, or a period of silence may be observed.

3. PRESENTATION OF THE CANDIDATES

After the readings the bishop (and the priests who assist him) are seated. The pastor or another priest, deacon, or catechist presents the candidates for confirmation according to the custom of the region. If possible, each candidate is called by name and comes individually to the sanctuary. If the candidates are children, they are accompanied by one of their sponsors or parents and both stand before the celebrant.

If there are many candidates, they are not called by name, but take a suitable place before the bishop.

4. HOMILY OR ADDRESS

The bishop then gives a brief homily. He should explain the readings and lead the candidates, their sponsors and parents, and the whole assembly to a deeper understanding of the mystery of confirmation.

He may use these or similar words:

BISHOP: At Pentecost the apostles received the Holy Spirit as the Lord had promised. They also received the power of giving the Holy Spirit and so completing the work of baptism. This we read in the Acts of the Apostles. When Saint Paul placed his hands on those who had been baptized, the Holy Spirit came upon them, and they began to speak in other languages and prophetic words.

Bishops are successors of the apostles and have this power of giving the Holy Spirit to the baptized, either personally or through the priests they appoint.

In our day the coming of the Holy Spirit is not usually marked by the gift of tongues, but we know his coming by faith. He fills our hearts with the love of God, brings us together in one faith but different vocations, and works within us to make the Church one and holy.

The gift of the Holy Spirit which you are to receive will be a spiritual sign and seal to make you more Christ-like and more perfect members of his Church. At his baptism by John, Christ was anointed by the Spirit and sent out on his public ministry to set the world on fire.

You have already been baptized into Christ and now you will receive the power of his Spirit and the sign of the cross on your forehead. You must be witnesses before all the world to his suffering, death, and resurrection; your way of life should reflect the goodness of Christ. Christ gives varied gifts to his Church, and the Spirit distributes them among the members of Christ's body to build up the holy people of God in unity and love.

Be active members of the Church, alive in Jesus Christ. Under the guidance of the Holy Spirit give your lives completely in the service of all, as did Christ, who came not to be served but to serve.

Before you receive the Spirit, renew the profession of faith you made in baptism or your parents and godparents made in union with the whole Church.

5. RENEWAL OF BAPTISMAL PROMISES

After the homily the candidates stand and the bishop questions them. They respond together.

BISHOP: Do you reject Satan and all his works and all his empty promises?

CANDIDATES: *I do.*

BISHOP: Do you believe in God the Father almighty, creator of heaven and earth?

CANDIDATES: *I do.*

BISHOP: Do you believe in Jesus Christ, his only Son, our Lord, who was born of the Virgin Mary, was crucified, died, and was buried, rose from the dead, and is now seated at the right hand of the Father?

CANDIDATES: *I do.*

BISHOP: Do you believe in the Holy Spirit, the Lord, the giver of life, who came to the apostles at Pentecost and who comes to you today in the sacrament of confirmation?

CANDIDATES: *I do.*

BISHOP: Do you believe in the holy catholic Church, the communion of saints, the forgiveness of sins, the resurrection of the body, and life everlasting?

CANDIDATES: *I do.*

The bishop then gives his assent to their profession of faith and proclaims the faith of the Church.

BISHOP: This is our faith. This is the faith of the Church. We are proud to profess it in Christ Jesus our Lord.

PEOPLE: *Amen.*

(For *This is our faith,* some other formula may be substituted, or the community may express its faith in a suitable song.)

6. IMPOSITION OF HANDS

While the priests who assist the bishop stand near him, he stands facing the people, and with hands joined, sings or says.

BISHOP: My dear friends: by baptism God our Father gave these adopted children new birth to eternal life. Let us ask him to pour out the Holy Spirit upon them, to strengthen them in their faith, and anoint them to be more like Christ the Son of God.

(All pray in silence for a short time.)

The bishop and the priests who assist him place their hands upon all the candidates. The bishop alone sings or says:

BISHOP: All-powerful God, Father of our Lord Jesus Christ, by water and the Holy Spirit you freed these candidates from sin. Send your Holy Spirit upon them to be their Helper and Guide. Give them the spirit of wisdom and understanding, the spirit of right judgment and courage, the spirit of knowledge and love, the spirit of reverence in your service. [We ask this] through Christ our Lord.*

PEOPLE: *Amen.*

7. ANOINTING

The deacon brings the chrism to the bishop. Each candidate goes to the bishop, or the bishop may go to the individual candidates. The one who presented the candidate places his right hand on the latter's shoulder and gives the candidate's name to the bishop; the candidate, however, may give his own name.

The bishop moistens his right thumb with chrism and makes the sign of the cross on the forehead of the one to be confirmed as he says:

BISHOP: N., receive the seal of the Holy Spirit, the Gift of the Father.

NEWLY-CONFIRMED: *Amen.*

BISHOP: Peace be with you.

NEWLY-CONFIRMED: *And also with you.*

---

*If there are several persons to be confirmed, the bishop may choose to extend his hands in a symbolic gesture of imposing hands. This imposition is not the sign of confirmation; it is a sign of invocation, as the accompanying prayer indicates.

If priests assist the bishop in conferring the sacrament, all the vessels of chrism are brought to the bishop by the deacon or by other ministers. The bishop gives a vessel of chrism to each of the priests.

The candidates go to the bishop or to the priests, or the bishop and priests may go to the candidates. The anointing is done as described above.

During the anointing a suitable song may be sung. After the anointing the bishop and the priests wash their hands.

8. GENERAL INTERCESSIONS

The general intercessions follow, in this or a similar form determined by the competent authority.

BISHOP: My brothers and sisters: let us be one in prayer to God our Father as we are one in faith, hope, and love his Spirit gives.

DEACON OR MINISTER: For our brothers and sisters, confirmed by the gift of the Spirit, that with faith and love as the foundation of their lives they may be witnesses to Christ the Lord. Let us pray to the Lord.

PEOPLE: *Lord, hear our prayer.*

DEACON OR MINISTER: For the parents and godparents who brought these newly-confirmed to the faith, that by word and example they may encourage them to follow the way of Jesus Christ. Let us pray to the Lord.

PEOPLE: *Lord, hear our prayer.*

DEACON OR MINISTER: For the holy Church of God, in union with N., our pope, N., our bishop, and all the bishops, that God, who gathers us together by the Holy Spirit, may help us to grow in unity of faith and love until his Son returns in glory. Let us pray to the Lord.

PEOPLE: *Lord, hear our prayer.*

DEACON OR MINISTER: For the whole world, that all who have but one Father, one Maker, may see beyond racial and national differences to their common brotherhood, and seek the kingdom of God in the peace of the Holy Spirit. Let us pray to the Lord.

PEOPLE: *Lord, hear our prayer.*

BISHOP: God our Father, you sent the Holy Spirit upon the apostles and through them and their successors you give the Spirit to your people. May the faith and love that spread everywhere when the gospel was first preached continue to grow through the hearts of all who believe. [We ask this] through Christ our Lord.

PEOPLE: *Amen.*

9. LORD'S PRAYER

All then say the Lord's Prayer, which the bishop may introduce in these or similar words.

BISHOP: Dear friends in Christ, let us pray together as the Lord Jesus Christ has taught.

PEOPLE: *Our Father, who art in heaven, hallowed be thy name; thy kingdom come; thy will be done on earth as it is in heaven. Give us this day our daily bread; and forgive us our trespasses as we forgive those who trespass against us; and lead us not into temptation, but deliver us from evil.*

10. BLESSING

After the Lord's Prayer the bishop blesses all present. In place of the usual blessing, the following blessing or prayer over the people is used.

The deacon or minister gives the invitation in these or similar words: "Bow your heads and pray for God's blessing."

The bishop extends his hands over the people and sings or says:

BISHOP: God our Father made you his children by water and the Holy Spirit: may he bless you and watch over you with his love.

PEOPLE: *Amen.*

BISHOP: Jesus Christ the Son of God has promised that the Spirit of truth will be with his Church for ever: may he bless you and give you courage to profess the true faith.

PEOPLE: *Amen.*

BISHOP: The Holy Spirit descended upon the first disciples and filled their hearts with love: may he bless you, keep you in faith and love, and bring you to the joy of the kingdom of God.

PEOPLE: *Amen.*

BISHOP: And may almighty God bless you, the Father, and the Son, ✠ and the Holy Spirit.

PEOPLE: *Amen.*

An appropriate hymn may be sung during which the bishop and the ministers recess to a suitable place to greet the newly confirmed.

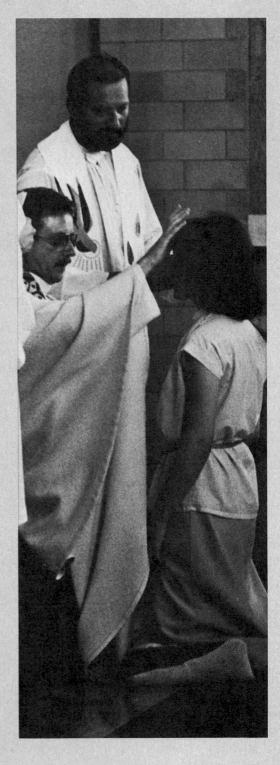

What does the Church celebrate in the Sacrament of Confirmaton? Why is it an initiation sacrament?

What is Confirmation a sign of?

Find out what you can about the oil used in Confirmation. What does it symbolize?

Your book speaks of the "duties and responsibilities of being a Christian." List four that you think are rather important.

Why are baptismal promises renewed during Confirmation?

In part 5 of the "Rite of Confirmation" the bishop speaks of "our faith." In your own words, tell what you think are the essentials of your Catholic faith.

What are the matter, form, and essential actions of the Sacrament of Confirmation?

What is the mission of the Holy Spirit in the world? Who is responsible for carrying out that mission? Why is this so?

Read the Acts of the Apostles, chapter 2. Be prepared to tell what things are described there.

Who is the bishop of your diocese?

Conclusion

Christians are lucky. They have been selected by God for a special kind of relationship with Him. This relationship is begun in the Sacrament of Baptism and sealed in the Sacrament of Confirmation. The gifts and privileges of God given with these sacraments are not for the individual Christian alone, however. They are given for the world. Each Christian is called by God to bring the good news of Jesus to those who do not have it. By their words and their actions Christians are either positive signs of the Spirit of Jesus at work, or they are negative signs that turn people away from Christ. Which are you at this stage of your life?

Summary

Through the liturgy, Catholics express a special kind of relationship with God and He expresses a special kind of relationship with them.

The sacraments are the principal acts of the liturgy.

The sacraments are signs of a Divine Reality taking place in an individual.

The special relationship that Christians enjoy with God begins in Baptism which is a sign of the Divine Life present in the Christian.

Confirmation is a sign that the special relationship that Christians have with God is sealed by the presence of the Holy Spirit.

Words You Should Know

Be sure that you can define the words given below. If you are in doubt about any, consult the Word List on page 234.

baptismal font	form	Paraclete
catechumens	homily	realm
compel	inherent	sacramental
covenant	matter	social dimension
efficacy		

For Review, Discussion, Research, and Reflection

1. If a friend asked you what a sacrament is, what would you say? Can you name the sacraments of the Catholic Church and tell what each is in brief?

2. What does your book mean by saying that the sacraments are part of the total sanctifying process? How does each fit into the process? Are the sacraments the only things that constitute the sanctifying process? Why? Why not?

3. Why, and in what way, is the Church the body of Christ? In your own words, give what you understand to be the mission of the Church in the world.

4. What three things about God's action are celebrated in each sacrament? What you do understand by each?

5. Why do we say that the sacraments have a social as well as a personal effect?

6. Your book uses words like matter, form, rite, sign, reality, moment, and continuous with regard to the sacraments. What does each mean in reference to Baptism and Confirmation?

7. What is Baptism a sign of? What is the essential action of the Sacrament of Baptism? What is its transforming aspect?

8. What is the Sacrament of Confirmation? What is the essential aspect of this sacrament? Do you think that people understand the nature and importance of the Sacrament of Confirmation? Why? Why not?

9. In your New Testament, read Galatians 5:13-25. Reflect on what St. Paul calls "the fruit of the Spirit."

10. On a separate sheet of paper, compose a prayer to the Holy Spirit.

11. In your New Testament, read 2 Timothy 1:6-8 and reflect on its meaning in your life. Name some ways in which his exhortation can be carried out in your life at this stage of your maturity.

12. Find out when you were baptized, where, and by whom. If you have been confirmed, when and where did it take place?

Nourishing the Special Relationship with God: the Eucharist

From the earliest days of Christianity, the Eucharistic action has been the center of the Church's life. It has been the supreme prayer and act of worship, the most important occasion of Christian instruction, the source of unity and love in the community. All other sacraments point toward the Eucharist and find their own fulfillment in it. The Eucharist is truly the center and the epitome of Christianity.

—Bernard Cooke

5.1 What the Sacrament of the Eucharist Is

As you know, people come together to worship God in various ways. Hindus, Moslems, Jews, Buddhists, Unitarians, Latter Day Saints, and so on, have worship services which express for them their worship-relationship with God. Christians assemble together to worship

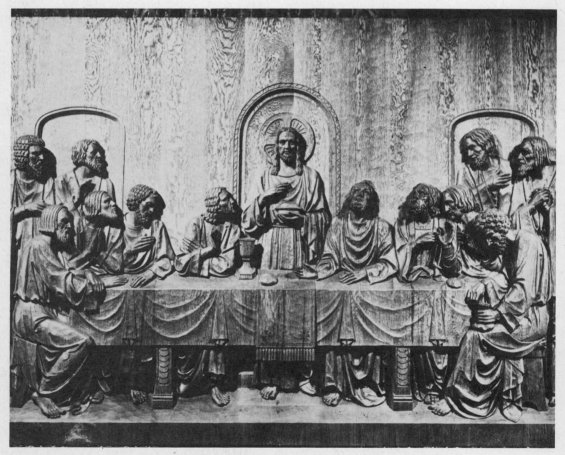

The Last Supper–a wood-carving by Alois Lang

God in various ways also. Catholic Christians worship God in the Mass as the Catholic community's proper, significant, and principal act of worship.

The liturgical action which American Catholics call "The Mass" is more properly called "The Eucharistic Liturgy," "The Sacrament of the Eucharist," or "The Lord's Supper." It is properly called "The Lord's Supper" because it is a memorial and reenactment of the Passover meal Jesus celebrated with his Apostles just before he died. It is called "The Eucharistic Liturgy" because of the solemn prayers of thanksgiving which became a part of the liturgical action of the Lord's Supper.*

It is called "The Mass" in English because a popular Latin term for the services surrounding the Lord's Supper was *missarum solemnia.*** This was shortened to *missa,* and became *masse* in Medieval English (about 1200–1400 A.D.) when languages were changing. Eventually it became "Mass" and finally "The Mass" by which it is popularly known today.

You have attended Mass literally hundreds of times, and you have studied it off and on for the past several years. It is not necessary, therefore, to go over every part of the Mass as if it were all new to you. What is important, however, is for you to understand exactly what the Mass is so that you can attend it as a mature Christian.

The Mass is a sign of the New Covenant with God which Jesus established at the Last Supper. (See Luke 22:19, 20.) **It is a sacramental meal which recalls the events of the Last Supper and makes present the risen Jesus in the assembly of his people.**

As you know, Noah, Abraham, and Moses established covenants with God.* So did Jesus. He changed the meaning and the substance of the Jewish Passover meal to a new covenant with God and gave his body and blood as a pledge of this covenant. He asked that his followers memorialize his action and make present this new covenant in their fellowship meetings. These meetings eventually became the solemn Eucharistic liturgy which Catholics celebrate all over the world every Sunday.

With this new covenant in his body and blood, Jesus established a special kind of relationship with God for his followers and gave them a means to sustain and nourish it.

The Eucharist is one of the initiation sacraments of the Catholic Church because once a person becomes a follower of Jesus in the Catholic Church, he or she is invited to share the body and blood of Jesus in fellowship with other Catholics.

---

*Eucharist comes from the Greek *eucharistia* meaning thankfulness or grateful.

**Missarum solemnia,* according to Joseph Martos in *Doors to the Sacred* (New York, Doubleday, 1981, page 252) was the dismissal ceremony of the early Eucharistic services which sent away, or dismissed, the catechumens and certain penitents from the solemn ceremonies of the Eucharistic liturgy which were celebrated only by Christians in good standing.

---

*See Genesis 9 and 15 and Exodus 19.

> FOR IT IS THROUGH THE LITURGY, ESPECIALLY THE DIVINE EUCHARISTIC SACRIFICE, THAT "THE WORK OF OUR REDEMPTION IS ACCOMPLISHED." THE LITURGY IS THUS THE OUTSTANDING MEANS BY WHICH THE FAITHFUL CAN EXPRESS IN THEIR LIVES, AND MANIFEST TO OTHERS, THE MYSTERY OF CHRIST AND THE REAL NATURE OF THE TRUE CHURCH.
>
> ~ Constitution on the Sacred Liturgy #2

5.2 The Unity of the Mass

The liturgy of the Eucharist is one sacramental action with two equal parts: The Liturgy of the Word and the Liturgy of the Eucharist. The central action of the Liturgy of the Word is the reading of Scripture. The central action of the Liturgy of the Eucharist is the receiving of the body and blood of Christ made present by the words of consecration.

The Liturgy of the Word has three parts: the Introductory Rites, the Readings, and the Prayers of the People. The Introductory Rites set the mood of the Mass and proclaim the theme or subject matter of the Mass. The Readings proclaim the revelation of God in both the Old and the New Testaments in keeping with the theme of the Mass and the role of Jesus in God's plans for His people. The Prayers of the People proclaim the needs of the community at Mass and petition the Father to hear the prayers.

The Creed proclaims the faith of the people and serves as a link between the two parts of the sacramental action.

The Liturgy of the Eucharist has three parts also: the Preparation, the Communion Rite, and the Concluding Rite. The Preparation contains the offertory in which the gifts are brought to the table of the Lord. It also has the Eucharistic Prayer in which the words of Jesus at the Last Supper are proclaimed. The Preparation ends with the community's "Great Amen"—its affirmation of the mystery of Christ presented in the Eucharistic Prayer.

The Communion Rite begins with the prayer Jesus taught his followers, the Lord's Prayer. This is followed with the sign of peace by which Christians proclaim their oneness in Jesus, their community fellowship, and their joy in the Lord. The reception of the body and blood of Christ in what we call the "communion" is the highlight of the Liturgy of the Eucharist.

The Concluding Rite contains the blessing of the community by its chosen minister, the proclamation of the conclusion of the Eucharistic Liturgy, and a reminder that the presence of Christ, experienced in the Eucharistic Liturgy, is to be made present in the world by Christian action.

The matter and form of the Liturgy of the Word are the reading of the Holy Scripture and the people's responses. The matter and form of the Liturgy of the Eucharist are the body and blood of Christ and the reception of communion. In both, the matter and form signify and are what they appear to be: nourishment for sustaining the special relationship that Christians have with God.*

The rituals of the Mass are those approved for various times and various places by the Church. They reflect the nature of the sacramental action, the solemnity of the worship, and the culture of the people assembled in the name of the Lord.

---

*Almost all Protestant groups celebrate the Eucharist—or Lord's Supper, as most of them call it—in one way or another. Some are very close to the Catholic way of celebrating; some are not. All, however proclaim the Word in Scripture and have at least a memorial of the Last Supper.

The Mass: One Sacramental Action

I. Introductory Rites

The procession
The prayer
The song of praise

II. The Scripture

The first reading
The second reading
The Gospel
The homily

III. The Prayers of the People

The prayer of the faithful

Creed

IV. The Preparation

The offertory
The Eucharistic prayer
The concluding acclamation

V. The Communion Rite

The Lord's prayer
The rite of peace
The communion

VI. The Concluding Rite

The blessing
The dismissal
The living of the Mass

Liturgy of the Word   **Liturgy of the Eucharist**

On the following pages is "The Order of Mass for Thanksgiving Day." Go over it carefully, then answer the following questions on another sheet of paper. Read the questions before you read the Rite.

1. What is the theme of the Mass given in this section? Mention three places where this theme is carried out.

2. Why is the first reading appropriate to this Mass?

3. What would you expect the homily to be about? If you were asked to give it, what three things would you stress?

4. What is the purpose of the offertory in any Mass? What do you see in this Mass that might be different from the offertory as you usually experience it?

5. In what early part of the Eucharistic Prayer is the meaning of the word eucharist brought out?

6. What besides the consecration is mentioned in the Eucharistic Prayer?

7. To what are the people responding in "The Great Amen"?

8. Read Luke 24:13-35. How did the disciples recognize Jesus? Why would this term be applicable to the Eucharistic Liturgy?

9. Look up the word "host" in the dictionary. Why is it a good name for the wafer received at communion?

10. If you had a chance, what prayer would you offer at the Prayer of the Faithful in this Mass?

As you know, the Mass has changed over the course of the history of the Church. Ask your parents or grandparents what the Mass was like when they were your age.

Look up the references to Noah, Abraham, and Moses. Be prepared to say what the covenant was and why it took place.

Read the reference to the Gospel according to Luke given on page 150. Memorize the words of consecration.

The Order of Mass for Thanksgiving Day

1. INTRODUCTORY RITE

When all are assembled, the entrance procession begins. The Commentator says:

COMMENTATOR: United States citizens have cherished Thanksgiving Day as a civil and religious festival since its institution by Governor William Bradford of Plymouth Colony in 1621. This custom spread throughout the British North American Colonies. During the Revolutionary War the Continental Congress adopted it, and the states observed the day thereafter. President Abraham Lincoln designated it a national holiday. A joint resolution of Congress in 1941 fixed the fourth Thursday of November as the national day of thanksgiving.

We gather as a worshipping community to thank God for His blessing on us as a community and as a nation. Joined together as the people of God in Christ, we begin this celebration of Thanksgiving Day with the song "Now Thank We All Our God."

Now thank we all our God
With heart and hands and voices;
Who wondrous things has done
In whom His world rejoices;
Who from our mother's arms
Has blessed us on our way
With countless gifts of love
And still is ours today.

O may this bounteous God
Through all our life be near us!
With ever joyful hearts
And blessed peace to cheer us.
And keep us in His grace
And guide us when perplexed
And free us from all ills
In this world and the next.

After the entrance song, all make the sign of the cross:

PRIEST: In the name of the Father, and of the Son, and of the Holy Spirit.

PEOPLE: *Amen.*

PRIEST: The grace of our Lord Jesus Christ and the love of God and the fellowship of the Holy Spirit be with you all.

PEOPLE: *And also with you.*

PRIEST: Dearly beloved friends in Christ, to prepare ourselves to celebrate the Sacred Eucharist, let us call to mind our sins and ask God to purify us with His loving forgiveness.

After an appropriate pause, the priest says:

PRIEST: Lord, we have sinned against you. Lord, have mercy.

PEOPLE: *Lord, have mercy.*

PRIEST: Lord, show us your mercy and love.

PEOPLE: *And grant us your salvation.*

PRIEST: May almighty God have mercy on us, forgive us our sins, and bring us to everlasting life.

PEOPLE: *Amen.*

COMMENTATOR: As the Church assembled in the Spirit to thank God for His blessings on us and on our country, let us praise God for His goodness in Christ.

PEOPLE:

> *Glory to God in the highest and peace to his people on earth.*
> *Lord God, heavenly King, almighty God and Father, we worship you, we give you thanks we praise you for your glory.*
> *Lord Jesus Christ, only Son of the Father,*
> *Lord God, Lamb of God, you take away the sin of the world:*
> *have mercy on us;*
> *you are seated at the right hand of the Father: receive our prayer.*
> *For you alone are the Holy One,*
> *you alone are the Lord,*
> *you alone are the Most High,*
> *Jesus Christ, with the Holy Spirit, in the glory of God the Father.*
> *Amen.*

The priest invites all to pray silently for a moment and then, in our name, expresses the theme of the day's celebration and petitions God the Father through the mediation of Christ in the Holy Spirit.

PRIEST: Let us pray.

Priest and people pray silently for a while. Then the priest says the opening prayer:

O God, you have fulfilled our founding fathers' faith in your divine providence by making and keeping us a land rich in the abundance of your creation.

Freedom, justice, and universal brotherhood are for us our precious heritage, but for countless men, in our midst and all over the world, they are still only a dream.

May we be faithful to share this heritage with the living and transmit it to a people still unborn:

through Jesus Christ.

PEOPLE: *Amen.*

2. THE LITURGY OF THE WORD

All sit.

COMMENTATOR: The proclamation of God's word is always centered on Christ, God's Word to people. Old Testament writings prepare for him; New Testament writings speak of him directly. Let us listen to God speaking to us reminding us of His care for His people in the past so that we shall maintain our confidence in His care for us and our country in the present.

READER: This reading is taken from the Book of Deuteronomy, chapter 8, verses 7 to 18.

Moses spoke to the people saying: "The Lord, your God, is bringing you into a good country, a land with streams of water, with springs and fountains welling up in the hills and valleys, and land of wheat and barley, of vines and fig trees and pomegranates, of olive trees and honey, a land where you can eat bread without stint and where you will lack nothing, a land whose stones contain iron and in whose hills you can mine copper. But when you have eaten your fill, you must bless the Lord, your God, for the good country he has given you. Be careful not to forget the Lord, your God, by neglecting his commandments and decrees and statutes which I enjoin on you today: lest when

148

you have eaten your fill, and you have built fine houses and lived in them, and have increased your herds and flocks, your silver and gold, and all your property, you then become haughty of heart and unmindful of the Lord, your God, who brought you out of the land of Egypt, that place of slavery; who guided you through the vast and terrible desert with its saraph serpents and scorpions, its parched and waterless ground; who brought forth water for you from the flinty rock and fed you in the desert with manna, a food unknown to your fathers, that he might afflict you and test you, but also make you prosperous in the end. Otherwise you might say to yourselves, 'It is my own power and the strength of my own hand that has obtained for me this wealth. Remember then, it is the Lord, your God, who gives you the power to acquire wealth, by fulfilling as he has now done, the covenant he swore to your fathers."

This is the word of the Lord.

PEOPLE: *Thanks be to God.*

COMMENTATOR: Let us reflect on God's goodness to us as we respond to the hymn of thanks from Psalm 138 by saying "I will give thanks to your name, because of your kindness and your truth."

READER: I will give thanks to you, O Lord, with all my heart,
   [for you have heard the words of my mouth;]
   in the presence of the angels I will sing your praise;
I will worship at your holy temple.

PEOPLE: *I will give thanks to your name, because of your kindness and your truth.*

READER: I will give thanks to your name, because of your kindness and your truth;
For you have made great above all things your name and your promise.
When I called, you answered me;
   you built up strength within me.

PEOPLE: *I will give thanks to your name, because of your kindness and your truth.*

READER: All the kings of the earth
shall give thanks to you, O Lord,
    when they hear the words of your mouth;
And they shall sing of the ways of the Lord:
    "Great is the glory of the Lord."

PEOPLE: *I will give thanks to your name,
because of your kindness and your truth.*

READER: This second reading is taken from St. Paul's First Letter to the Corinthians, chapter 1, verses 4 to 9.

I always give thanks to my God for you, because of the grace he has given you through Christ Jesus. For in union with Christ you have become rich in all things, including all speech and all knowledge. The message about Christ has become so firmly fixed in you, that you have not failed to receive a single blessing, as you wait for our Lord Jesus Christ to be revealed. He will also keep you firm to the end, so that you will be found without fault in the Day of our Lord Jesus Christ. God is to be trusted, the God who called you to have fellowship with his Son Jesus Christ, our Lord.

This is the word of the Lord.

PEOPLE: *Thanks be to God.*

All stand.

COMMENTATOR: Because Jesus will speak to us in his gospel, let us stand and prepare ourselves to receive his word by responding to St. Paul's words of praise to God the Father by saying "Alleluia."

READER: Blessed be God, the Father of our Lord Jesus Christ who has blessed us with all spiritual blessings of heaven in Christ.

PEOPLE: *Alleluia.*

The priest, as the proper minister, now reads the Gospel.

PRIEST: A reading from the holy Gospel according to Luke.

PEOPLE: *Glory to you, Lord.*

PRIEST: Jesus said to the crowd, "Watch and be on your guard against all kinds of greed; for a man's true life is not made up of the things he owns, no matter how rich he may be." Then Jesus told them this parable: "A rich man had land which bore good crops. He began to think to himself, 'I don't have a place to keep all my crops. What can I do? This is what I will do,' he told himself; 'I will tear my barns down and build bigger ones, where I will store the grain and all my other goods. Then I will say to myself: Lucky man! You have all the good things you need for many years. Take life easy, eat, drink, and enjoy yourself!' But God said to him, 'You fool! This very night you will have to give up your life; then who will get all these things you have kept for yourself?' " And Jesus concluded, "This is how it is with those who pile up riches for themselves but are not rich in God's sight."

This is the gospel of the Lord.

PEOPLE: *Praise to you, Lord Jesus Christ.*

The Liturgy of the Word is concluded with a homily, which is an explanation of the meaning of the words of Jesus as they apply to modern times, and the "General Intercessions," during which the people pray for the general needs of the Church, for the needs of the world, the country, the city or town, and the parish.

After the homily, the priest says:

PRIEST: Let us together thank God for all His blessings, and let us pray for all those who do not enjoy either our freedom or our natural goods.

COMMENTATOR: The response to the petitions is, "We thank you, Lord our God."

The petitions are given by the priest, the commentator, the reader, some other minister, or anyone from the congregation. They might be like the following:

• That the Church may always seek God's kingdom and His will, we pray to the Lord.
• That all Catholic Christians may join in praising God for His blessings to our country, we pray to the Lord.
• That the President, the members of Congress, and all who serve in public office may be mindful of God's care for our country, we pray to the Lord.
• That we may always remember the good fortune each of us enjoys, we pray to the Lord.
• That the poor, the sick and the suffering may soon feel relief for their sufferings through the generosity of all Christians, we pray to the Lord.
• That God will bless our parish and send His Spirit to us so that we will fulfill our Christian mission, we pray to the Lord.

PRIEST: God our Father, you have blessed us all by calling us to live in freedom and prosperity in this land of ours. Keep us always mindful that it is you who sends good things to us so that we may make your good available to those who do not have them. Make us as generous in our lives as you are with us. Continue to bless our country and make us ministers of your peace throughout the world. We ask this through Christ our Lord.

PEOPLE: *Amen.*

3. LITURGY OF THE EUCHARIST

A. *The Offertory*

All sit.

COMMENTATOR: Made ready by reflection on God's Word, we begin now the Eucharistic sacrifice itself, the Supper of the Lord. We celebrate the memorial which the Lord instituted at his Last Supper. As God's people, the redeemed brothers of Christ, gathered by him around his table, we are here to bless God and to receive the gift of Jesus' body and blood so that our faith and life may be transformed.

The bread and wine for the Eucharist, with our gifts for the Church and the poor, are gathered and brought to the altar. We prepare our hearts by song or in silence as the Lord's table is being set.

While the gifts of the people are brought forward to the priest and are placed on the altar, the offertory hymn is sung.

Before placing the bread on the altar, the priest says quietly:

Blessed are you, Lord, God of all creation. Through your goodness we have this bread to offer, which earth has given and human hands have made. It will become for us the bread of life.

If there is no singing, the priest may say this prayer aloud, and the people may respond:

Blessed be God for ever.

When he pours wine and a little water into the chalice, the deacon (or the priest) says quietly:

By the mystery of this water and wine may we come to share in the divinity of Christ, who humbled himself to share in our humanity.

Before placing the chalice on the altar, the priest says quietly:

Blessed are you, Lord, God of all creation. Through your goodness we have this wine to offer, fruit of the vine and work of human hands. It will become our spiritual drink.

If there is no singing, the priest may say this prayer aloud, and the people may respond:

Blessed be God for ever.

The priest says quietly:

Lord God, we ask you to receive us and be pleased with the sacrifice we offer you with humble and contrite hearts.

Then he washes his hands, saying quietly:

Lord, wash away my iniquity; cleanse me from my sin.

When the gifts are prepared and the materials of the Eucharist are ready, the priest invites all present to join with him in prayer.

PRIEST: Pray, brethren, that our sacrifice may be acceptable to God, the almighty Father.

PEOPLE: *May the Lord accept the sacrifice at your hands, for the praise and glory of his name, for our good, and the good of all his Church.*

After all have prayed together, the priest says "The Prayer Over the Gifts," summarizing in the official prayer of the Church the meaning of the feast being celebrated.

PRIEST: God our Father, all good things have come to us from your hand, and you have made us stewards of the richness of the earth. Accept these offerings of bread and wine as a sign that we wish to share the blessings of the Holy Table and the banquet of life with all our brothers in the human family: through Christ our Lord.

PEOPLE: *Amen.*

B. The Eucharistic Prayer

All kneel, stand, or sit.

COMMENTATOR: We begin the Eucharistic service of praise and thanksgiving, the center of the entire celebration, the central prayer of worship. At the priest's invitation we lift our hearts to God and unite with him in the words he addresses to the Father through Jesus Christ. Together we join Christ in his sacrifice, celebrating his memorial in the holy meal and acknowledging with him the wonderful works of God in our lives.

PRIEST: The Lord be with you.

PEOPLE: *And also with you.*

PRIEST: Lift up your hearts.

PEOPLE: *We lift them up to the Lord.*

PRIEST: Let us give thanks to the Lord our God.

PEOPLE: *It is right to give him thanks and praise.*

PRIEST: Father, all-powerful and ever-living God, we do well always and everywhere to give you thanks through Jesus Christ our Lord.
You made man to your own image and set him over all creation.
Once you chose a people and gave them a destiny and, when you brought them out of the bondage to freedom they carried with them the promise that all men would be blessed and all men could be free.

What the prophets pledged was fulfilled in Jesus Christ, your Son and our saving Lord.

It has come to pass in every generation for all men who have believed that Jesus, by his death and resurrection, gave them a new freedom in his Spirit.

It happened to our fathers, who came to this land as if out of the desert into a place of promise and hope.

It happens to us still, in our time, as you lead all men through your Church to the blessed vision of peace.

And so, with all the multitude of angels in the heavenly court, we proclaim your glory as we join in their unending hymn:

The priest and the people together say:

Holy, holy, holy Lord, God of power and might, heaven and earth are full of your glory.
Hosanna in the highest.
Blessed is he who comes in the name of the Lord.
Hosanna in the highest.

The priest then says the prayer which contains the Consecration. Immediately after the Consecration, the people affirm their belief in the risen Christ with the "Memorial Acclamation." There are four different Eucharistic prayers, any one of which may be used in various Masses. Only one is given here.

PRIEST: We come to you, Father, with praise and thanksgiving, through Jesus Christ your Son.

Through him we ask you to accept and bless these gifts we offer you in sacrifice.

We offer them for your holy catholic Church, watch over it, Lord, and guide it; grant it peace and unity throughout the world.

We offer them for N., our Pope, for N., our bishop,
and for all who hold and teach the catholic faith that comes to us from the apostles.

Remember, Lord, your people,
especially those for whom we now pray, N. and
   N.
Remember all of us gathered here before you.
You know how firmly we believe in you and
   dedicate ourselves to you.
We offer you this sacrifice of praise for
   ourselves and those who are dear to us.
We pray to you, our living and true God, for
   our well-being and redemption.
In union with the whole Church we honor
   Mary, the ever-virgin mother of Jesus Christ
   our Lord and God.
We honor Joseph, her husband, the apostles and
   martyrs Peter and Paul, Andrew, [James,
   John, Thomas, James, Philip, Bartholomew,
   Matthew, Simon and Jude;
we honor Linus, Cletus, Clement, Sixtus,
   Cornelius, Cyprian, Lawrence, Chrysogonus,
   John and Paul, Cosmas and Damian] and all
   the saints.
May their merits and prayers gain us your
   constant help and protection.
Father, accept this offering from your whole
   family.
Grant us your peace in this life, save us from
   final damnation, and count us among those
   you have chosen.

Bless and approve our offering; make it
   acceptable to you, an offering in spirit and in
   truth.
Let it become for us the body and blood of
   Jesus Christ, your only Son, our Lord.

The day before he suffered
he took bread in his sacred hands
and looking up to heaven,
to you, his almighty Father,
he gave you thanks and praise.
He broke the bread,
gave it to his disciples, and said:
Take this, all of you, and eat it:
this is my body
which will be given up for you.

Here the priest holds the Bread for all to see.

When supper was ended,
he took the cup.
Again he gave you
thanks and praise,
gave the cup to his disciples,
and said: Take this, all of you,
and drink from it:
this is the cup of my blood,
the blood of the new
and everlasting covenant.
It will be shed for you
and for all
so that sins may be forgiven.
Do this in memory of me.

The priest holds the Chalice for all to see.

Let us proclaim the mystery of faith.

PEOPLE: *Christ has died,*
        Christ is risen,
        Christ will come again.

PRIEST: Father, we celebrate the memory of
Christ, your Son.
We, your people and your ministers, recall his
   passion, his resurrection from the dead, and
   his ascension into glory; and from the many
   gifts you have given us we offer to you, God
   of glory and majesty, this holy and perfect
   sacrifice: the bread of life and the cup of
   eternal salvation.
Look with favor on these offerings and accept
   them as once you accepted the gifts of your
   servant Abel, the sacrifice of Abraham, our
   father in faith, and the bread and wine
   offered by your priest Melchisedech.

Almighty God, we pray that your angel may take this sacrifice to your altar in heaven.

Then, as we receive from this altar the sacred body and blood of your Son, let us be filled with every grace and blessing.

Remember, Lord, those who have died and have gone before us marked with the sign of faith, especially those for whom we now pray, N. and N.

May these, and all who sleep in Christ, find in your presence light, happiness, and peace.

For ourselves, too, we ask some share in the fellowship of your apostles and martyrs, with John the Baptist, Stephen, Matthias, Barnabas, [other saints may be mentioned, including, N. our patron,] and all the saints.

Though we are sinners, we trust in your mercy and love.

Do not consider what we truly deserve, but grant us your forgiveness.

Through Christ our Lord you give us all these gifts.

You fill them with life and goodness, you bless them and make them holy.

Here the priest holds the chalice and the paten with the Host in such a way that all present may see them as he rises them both about eye level.

**Through him, with him,
in him, in the unity of the Holy Spirit,
all glory and honor is yours,
almighty Father, for ever and ever.**

PEOPLE: *Amen.*

4. THE COMMUNION RITE

The Eucharistic Prayer having been completed, the people are invited to accept Jesus' invitation to receive his body and blood. To prepare for this great banquet, we pray as our Lord prayed and signify our unity and brotherhood by exchanging a sign of peace and friendship with each other.

PRIEST: Let us pray with confidence to the Father in the words our Savior gave us:

PRIEST AND PEOPLE:
Our Father, who art in heaven,
hallowed be thy name;
thy kingdom come;
thy will be done on earth as it is in heaven.
Give us this day our daily bread;
and forgive us our trespasses
as we forgive those
who trespass against us;
and lead us not into temptation,
but deliver us from evil.

PRIEST: Deliver us, Lord, from every evil, and grant us peace in our day. In your mercy keep us free from sin and protect us from all anxiety as we wait in joyful hope for the coming of our Savior, Jesus Christ.

PEOPLE: *For the kingdom, the power, and the glory are yours, now and for ever.*

PRIEST: Lord Jesus Christ,
    you said to your apostles:
I leave you peace, my peace I give you.
Look not on our sins, but on the faith of your
    Church, and grant us the peace and unity of
    your kingdom where you live for ever and
    ever.

PEOPLE: *Amen.*

PRIEST: The peace of the Lord be with you always.

PEOPLE: *And also with you.*

PRIEST: Let us offer each other the sign of peace.

The people exchange a sign of peace and love, according to local custom.

Christians are gathered for "the breaking of the bread," another name for the Eucharist. To signify this breaking of the bread and the unity of all Christians in the receiving of the Eucharist, the priest breaks a small portion

from the Host and places it in the Chalice, saying:

May this mingling of the body and blood of our Lord Jesus Christ bring eternal life to us who receive it.

Meanwhile the people sing or say:
Lamb of God, you take away the sins of the world; have mercy on us.
Lamb of God, you take away the sins of the world: have mercy on us.
Lamb of God, you take away the sins of the world: grant us peace.

The preparation for Communion having been completed, the people are given an opportunity to receive the body and blood of Christ. During the Communion Service itself an appropriate song may be sung, but it should be in keeping with the meaning of Holy Communion, not just any song. If no song is sung, a Psalm or other Scripture may be recited by the people present. Before Communion the priest says quietly:

Lord Jesus Christ, Son of the living God, by the will of the Father and the work of the Holy Spirit, your death brought life to the world. By your holy body and blood, free me from all my sins and from every evil. Keep me faithful to your teaching, and never let me be parted from you.

Then he says aloud as he raises the Host for all to see:

This is the Lamb of God who takes away the sins of the world. Happy are those who are called to his supper.

Then the priest and the people say aloud together:

Lord, I am not worthy to receive you, but only say the word and I shall be healed.

Immediately before receiving Communion himself, the priest says quietly, "May the body of Christ bring me to everlasting life" (he takes the Host), and "May the blood of Christ bring me to everlasting life" (he takes the contents of the Chalice).

He then distributes Holy Communion to the people saying to each one as he presents the Host to them:

The Body of Christ.

To which each person replies:

Amen.

After Communion there is a period of silence and reflection. When this is completed, the priest invites all present to pray with him.

PRIEST: Let us pray. Thinking back on your boundless generosity as we share this thanksgiving meal, O Lord, we cannot fail to be reminded of our shortcomings towards others.

Let us share with generous hearts and open hands the fruits of the earth which you have given into our keeping as we hope to share the fruits of eternal life: through Christ our Lord.

5. THE CONCLUDING RITE

All stand.

COMMENTATOR: Having been reminded of our special blessings on this Thanksgiving Day and having received the body and blood of Christ as our nourishment, let us put into practice the lesson of our Eucharist by acting in love toward all we meet.

[Here any announcements appropriate to the day or the parish are made. After these the priest invokes God's blessing on all present.]

PRIEST: The Lord be with you.

PEOPLE: And also with you.

PRIEST: May almighty God bless you:
The Father, and the Son, and the Holy Spirit.

PEOPLE: Amen.

PRIEST: Go in peace to love and serve the Lord.

PEOPLE: Thanks be to God.

A hymn is sung in keeping with the theme of the day. It is appropriate to sing, for example, "God Bless America" as the priest and ministers leave the place of sacrifice.

5.4 The Presence of Jesus in the Sacrament of the Eucharist

The special relationship with God which Catholics believe they experience in the liturgy is best demonstrated in the Sacrament of the Eucharist.

It is best demonstrated in the Sacrament of the Eucharist because Catholics believe that the risen Jesus is sacramentally present on the altar under the *appearances* of bread and wine after the words of consecration are spoken. That is, they believe that Jesus is really present in the Eucharist "body and blood, soul and divinity," as it has often been phrased. They believe that in Communion they receive the body and blood of Christ.

This faith in the special presence of Jesus in the Eucharist comes to Catholics from the very first days of the Church. "The food which has been made eucharist through the prayer formed out of the words of Christ, and which nourishes and becomes our flesh and blood is the flesh and blood of the same Jesus who was made incarnate," wrote an early Christian writer.

This presence is different from his presence in his praying, worshipping community. It is different from his presence in an individual after Baptism. In each of these, his presence is appropriate to the sacramental action taking place. In the Eucharist, however, Jesus is present in a different manner. He is visibly, physically present under the appearances of bread and wine.

Christ of St. John of the Cross by Salvador Dali

The reality of the presence of Jesus in this specific form at this specific time is what "makes" the Mass. Without it, the Mass would simply be a memorial, an assembly of like-minded people, a gathering of "God's people" to hear His word proclaimed and explained, and a symbolic meal with only a symbolic significance. God would be present and Jesus would be acting in and through his people without the Consecration, it is true. But with it, Catholics experience a new dimension of God's action, and His presence becomes a reality: Jesus is truly present in his Risen Life.

5.5 Some Further Thoughts on What the Mass Is

Although the Mass stems from a remarkably simple action of Jesus (taking bread and wine and identifying himself with it), it has many meanings in addition to the ones given above. Among the more general meanings are the following.

A. Each Mass is a memorial, a reenactment, and a continued expression of the sacrifice Jesus offered to his Father for people.

When Jesus gave us his body and blood at the Last Supper, he said specifically that he was to die for the forgiveness of sins. (See Matthew 26:27, 28.) He said that his blood was to be "poured out" (in the manner of a sacrificial victim) so that people would be saved. The reference to sacrifice is so obvious that the Eucharist is a recalling and a renewal of the sacrifice of Jesus. In every Mass, this sacrifice of Jesus is made present and real. This is the symbolism of the separate consecrations of the bread ["my body"] and wine ["my blood"]. This is why the Mass is often called "The Eucharistic Sacrifice."

B. Each Mass is a sign of the present reality of the unity in Christ that exists among Catholic Christians.

There is a basic unity that exists among all Christians signified by their Baptism. It is a unity of faith in Jesus as savior. In addition to that, Catholic Christians

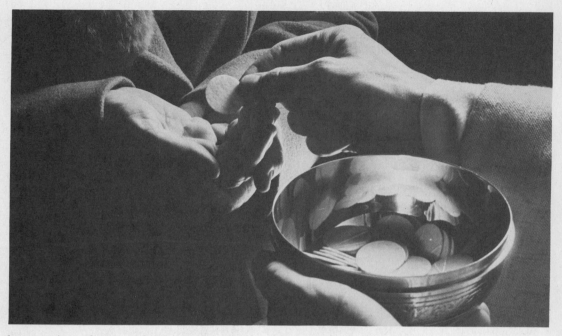

have a sign of unity of their own: a one-ness of worship.

In the Mass, Catholic Christians not only worship together in unity, however. They also receive together the body and blood of Christ, which unites them in a special way to Christ and to each other. In the Communion Rite, Catholic Christians become one body, not in theory, not simply spiritually, and not figuratively. They become one body in reality, as St. Paul reminded his Corinthian converts: "Is not the cup of blessing we bless a sharing in the blood of Christ? And is not the bread we break a sharing in the body of Christ? Because the loaf of bread is one, we, many though we are, are one body, for we all partake of the one loaf." (1 Corinthians 10:16–17)

But this sharing of the "one loaf" is more than a sign and a reality of union with Christ and each other. It is a sign and a reality of nourishment also. Celebrating the Eucharist together is not simply a gathering of interested Catholics. It is a meal shared together for nourishment— for the "food value" involved in eating the Eucharist. The food value is not in the amount taken. It is in what is taken and what it is: the body and blood of Christ taken for the spiritual nourishment of the individual and the community. Through the Eucharistic meal, Catholic Christians are nourished with the food they need–the Body of Christ. They receive the Life-giving nourishment of Christ. They share in reality in the Life of God. It is for this reason that the Eucharist is a sacrament. It is a real, personal, bodily encounter with Christ in his Church.

C. Each Mass is a celebration of the saving actions of God in Christ.

Christians believe that the whole purpose of creation—the reason for existence—is told and summed up in Christ.

In the Mass, Catholics recall not simply the reality of the "earthly" Jesus who existed in time in a particular place. They also recall and make present the reality of the risen Jesus who is made present to creation in his body, the Eucharist during Mass.

For this reason, the Mass is a celebration of the saving actions of God accomplished here and now in Christ in the lives of people who are being brought to their fulfillment (that is, are being saved) through Christ, who acts on them and in them in the sacramental life of the Church.

D. All other sacraments seem to be directly related to, and seem to be for, the Sacrament of the Eucharist.

The Mass, as we said earlier, is the great, central act of worship of the Roman Catholic Church. It is the worship of God in Christ. It is the people of God gathered to worship the Father with Christ at their head. It is the action which most perfectly expresses what the Church is for. It is the Church honoring the Father by offering His Christ to Him for His people.

It is for this act of worship that all other sacraments seem to prepare us. All of them are part of the sanctifying process that makes us worthy to participate in the worship of God under the headship of Christ in the Eucharistic Liturgy.

Baptism, for example, as a sign of our entrance into the community, prepares us for participation in the Eucharist. Confirmation enables us to participate fully in the action of the Spirit most perfectly expressed in the Eucharist. The Sacrament of Reconciliation, brings us into harmony with the community so that we can celebrate the Eucharist in love. Matrimony builds up the body of Christ for Eucharistic worship. Ordination designates the proper minister of the Eucharist who stands before the community to make present the Gift of God in the Eucharist. The Anointing of the Sick prepares the sick for entrance into the eternal Eucharistic community—the goal of Christian living, the purpose of redemption, and the fulfillment of God's plan for His Creation.

At the direction of your teacher, either answer the following questions on another sheet of paper, or be prepared to discuss them with your classmates in an open forum.

In "C" above, your book says, "Christians believe that the whole purpose of creation . . . is told and summed up in Christ." What does this mean? (Before answering, read the Gospel according to John 1:1–18.)

In "B" above, a statement is made about why the Eucharistic Liturgy is a sacrament. What is that statement?

How do the materials used in the Mass fulfill the requirements for materials used in any sacrament? (See page 96 to refresh your memory on this point.)

Why is the sign of peace given during Mass? What are people supposed to say to each other? How do you feel at that moment in the Mass?

How does the presence of Christ in the Eucharist differ from his other presences in the other sacraments and in his followers?

What is the meaning of the following words you say during Mass, "Christ has died, Christ is risen, Christ will come again"? When are they said?

Conclusion

The Christian community assembled for worship is a visible sign of God's saving actions in Jesus. Through the Church, God continues to reveal Himself in Jesus through the Liturgy of the Word and the Liturgy of the Eucharist, during which Jesus both confirms his covenant, and his people testify to their agreement to be his people. By becoming a living reality in the midst of his community, Jesus continues to reveal himself in time and give testimony to the love of God for His people.

Summary

The Mass is the Catholic Church's highest form of worship and most important sacrament.

The Mass is a sign of Christ's covenant with the Father and a sacramental meal in which Jesus is received whole and entire under the appearances of bread and wine.

Although the Mass has two principal and equal parts, it is one sacramental action because in it Catholics encounter God in Christ.

The mystery of Christ experienced in the Mass has many inexhaustible meanings. Aside from the obvious ones understood by everyone, there are many "private" meanings that stir the faith and the emotions of individuals. These, too, make the Mass meaningful.

Words You Should Know

Be sure that you can define the words given below. If there are any you are not sure of, consult the Word List on page 234.

| affirmation | memorialize | Passover |
| Father of the Church | | theme |

For Review, Discussion, Research, and Reflection

1. What is the Mass? What are other names for the Mass?

2. What are the principal parts of the Mass? Explain what each is. Be able to tell what occurs and in what order for each of the parts.

3. Discuss the significance of Jesus' establishing his new covenant at his "Last Supper."

4. Prepare a report on the Jewish Passover ceremony.

5. You sometimes hear some persons say that they don't go to Mass because they don't get anything out of it. Discuss this idea in light of what you now understand about the Mass.

6. Why can we say that the Mass is a unified action? Explain.

7. Prepare a report on the Eucharistic celebration in the early Church.

8. Why should a person receive Holy Communion when he celebrates Mass?

9. Do you think it is important and necessary to have some prescribed ritual for the celebration of the Eucharist? Why? Why not?

10. What is meant by the theme of a Mass? How is the theme of the Thanksgiving Mass given in your book carried out?

11. What do you think the theme of the following days might be in the Mass:

First Sunday of Advent

Easter

Pentecost

The feast of St. Joseph

Ash Wednesday

12. In what ways is the Mass a sign of the present reality of unity in Christ among Catholic Christians?

13. How are the other sacraments related to the Eucharist?

14. In your New Testament, read Ephesians 1:2-7. Discuss its central thought in light of the contents of this chapter in your book.

15. In light of your discussion of question 14, give what you think is the reason for Scripture readings at Mass. Why must one of the readings always be from the Gospels?

16. In an open forum discuss the problems your age group has with the Mass. Make some suggestions for responding to these problems.

17. At the direction of your teacher, select one part of the Mass and in conjunction with your classmates, prepare a Mass Rite for your class.

18. Reread the quotation that introduced this chapter and reflect on its meaning for the Church and for you personally.

19. Find out if any of your non-Catholic friends have a Eucharistic liturgy. If they do, ask them to explain what it is for them.

The Special Relationship with God and "The Healing Sacraments"

Listen to me, Lord, and answer
   me, for I am helpless and weak.
Save me from death, because I
   am loyal to you; save me, for I
   am your servant and I trust in
   you.
You are my God, so be merciful
   to me; I pray to you all day
   long.
Make your servant glad, O Lord,
   because my prayers go up to
   you.
You are good to us and forgiving,
   full of constant love for all who
   pray to you.
Listen, Lord, to my prayer; hear
   my cries for help.
I call to you in times of trouble,
   because you answer my
   prayers.

—Psalm 86:1–7

6.1 Evil in the World

It doesn't take a genius to know that
there are all kinds of evil, sin, and suffering in the world. America and Russia
maintain a wary posture toward each
other. The Arabs and the Israelis are
teetering on the brink of all-out war
that threatens to engulf the whole
world. Central America, South America,
Southeast Asia, the Middle East, and
parts of Africa are devastated by civil
war. People are killed and maimed, property destroyed and lives disrupted. Political terrorists in Italy, Germany, Spain,
and Ireland keep the flames of hatred
burning and destroy people's lives and
security to achieve their own selfish ends.

Millions of people throughout the world are starving to death, and millions more do not have adequate housing, water, or sanitation.

But these are global problems far removed from your life. Closer perhaps to your own experience, are the evils of poverty, social injustice, murder, assault, robbery, rape, and rioting which plague communities of all sizes. You, yourself, may have been the victim of hatred, fighting, stealing, lying, cheating, and a host of other things which are antisocial and antihuman. Every day you hear of older people and young children suffering abuse. You hear of people being the victims of rip-offs or gouging, of people being cheated or sold shoddy merchandise, and of con artists taking advantage of innocent men and women.

And haven't you experienced evil, sin, unpleasantness, and difficulty in your home, your school, and your neighborhood? Everyone has. We know that evil exists and we try to cope with it and live with it.

Not everyone is evil, of course (though we all have a tendency to do evil things), and we do experience more good than evil in our lives. The fact remains, however, that there is much evil in the world, in our country, in our neighborhoods, and in our own lives. Getting rid of it in ourselves is the first step in rooting it out of the world in which we live.

6.2 Jesus and the Power of Evil

The Gospels were "catechisms of the early Christian communities." They were written for those who already believed. Therefore, they not only proclaimed Jesus as savior, they also showed *how* he was savior. In other words, they taught the people. They showed the meaning of Jesus' saving presence in the world.

A perfect example of this Gospel-role in the early Church is found in the opening chapter, verse 15 of the Gospel according to Mark. In it Mark sets the tone and theme of his account of "the good news." "This is the time of fulfillment," he has Jesus saying. "The reign of God is at hand! Reform your lives and believe in the Gospel." Thus, in one verse, he gives the reason for and the purpose of Jesus'

coming into the world: "God is here," Mark says. "The power of evil is broken."

What does Mark mean by "the reign of God"? When the Gospel was written, power was in the hands of kings or emperors who ruled with absolute authority. Their philosophy of government, their laws, and their personal life-style set the tone and tempo of life for their subjects. What Mark is saying is that with the coming of Jesus, God entered directly into His creation and that from that time on, the tone and tempo of living should be guided by Jesus' philosophy of life, his laws, and his life-style.

In other words, with the coming of Jesus, Mark says, the ultimate evil—nondivine existence for creation—was overcome. What was left, he says, is the *effects* of ultimate evil—the physical, moral, spiritual, psychological, social, and economic evils that plague society. These, he said, needed to be rooted out of people's lives.

Jesus' Power over Evil

All the Gospels demonstrate the need for overcoming evil by showing Jesus overcoming evil through his words and his actions. They also stress Jesus' command to his followers to overcome evil in themselves and in the society in which they live.

In the first case, they show Jesus overcoming *physical* evils by working healing miracles. They show him overcoming *spiritual* evils by forgiving sin. They show him overcoming *psychological* evil by counseling and *social* evil by treating people with loving concern. They show

him overcoming *economic* evil by giving attention to the poor, the blind, the lame, the crippled, and the outcasts of his society.

In the second case, they stress Jesus' command that his followers work to overcome these same evils by leading lives of personal holiness and active love. A typical example of Jesus' insistence on love of neighbor is found in the Gospel according to Mark, chapter 12, verses 28 to 34.

A teacher of the Law . . . saw that Jesus had given the Sadducees a good answer, so he came to him with a question: "Which commandment is the most important of all?" "This is the most important one," said Jesus. " 'Hear, Israel! The Lord our God is the only Lord. You must love the Lord your God with all your heart, and with all your soul, and with all your mind, and with all your strength.' The second most important commandment is this: 'You must love your neighbor as yourself.' There is no other commandment more important than these two." The teacher of the Law said to Jesus: "Well done, Teacher! It is true, as you say, that only the Lord is God, and that there is no other god but he. And so man must love God with all his heart, and with all his mind, and with all his strength; and he must love his neighbor as himself. It is much better to obey these two commandments than to bring animals to be burned on the altar and offer other sacrifices to God."

Jesus noticed how wise his answer was, and so he told him: "You are not far from the Kingdom of God."

The Church, as the body of Christ in the world, expresses in its life the holiness of Jesus and his concern for overcoming evil. It pays careful attention to the social problems plaguing the world and advises its members on dealing with these problems. It also offers its members its "healing sacraments"—**The Sacrament of Reconciliation** and **The Anointing of the Sick.** The one reestablishes the special relationship with God if it should be lost in whole or in part. The other reminds sick people that the special relationship they have with God is strong, lasting, and eternal.

The Gospels are full of instances of Jesus overcoming evil. A few are listed below. Read the selections indicated and, on another sheet of paper, tell what the evil was that Jesus overcame. All the selections are from The Gospel According to Mark.

1:40–42	6:34–44
2:1–12	6:45–52
4:35–41	7:31–37
5:21–43	16:1–8

Find two examples of Jesus overcoming evil in each of the other Gospel accounts. Cite the reference and tell what evil Jesus overcomes.

Read the Gospel according to Luke, chapter 10, verses 25–37 to see what Jesus meant by "neighbor." Summarize the account.

Discuss in what sense all of us are sinners.

Give what you think are three major evils or sources of evil in your age group in your area. How do you think they can be offset?

Reestablishing the Special Relationship with God through the Sacrament of Reconciliation

and the New Testaments. God the creator, God the savior, God the Lord of history, salvation, and covenant are only a few. One of the dominant themes is that of the sinfulness of people and the gift of God's forgiveness. (See, for example, Psalm 6; Daniel 9:3–19; Luke 7:36–50; Matthew 9:9–13.) It is in this context of biblical revelation that the Church celebrates the Sacrament of Reconciliation.

The Sacrament of Reconciliation does not make sense unless a person understands the nature of moral evil and recognizes the existence of sin in himself, in others, and in the world.

Sin, by its nature, is an act, or a state, of alienation or separation from God and society. It is a turning away, partially or completely, from the end for which a person and society have been created. It is any deliberate action which is not the human thing to do in the circumstances in which a person finds himself.

There are many kinds of sin and many degrees of sinfulness. There are sins against God, such as blasphemy; sins against self, such as the indiscriminate use of drugs; and sins against others, such as stealing. There are individual sins, such as lying. There are family sins, such as fighting, arguing, or misuse of family funds. There are group sins, such as gang violence or vandalism, or corporate fraud.

There are social sins, such as discrimination or failure to help the poor. There are regional sins which involve a whole region or area, such as prejudice, and national sins involving a whole nation, such as an unjust war. There are world sins, such as the rape of natural resources or the unjustified pollution of the earth.

There are extremely serious sins, very serious sins, serious sins, and not-so-serious sins. There are individual acts of sin, habits of sin, and states of sin.

No one can deny that moral evil and sin exist in the world, and that moral evil and sin are harmful to individuals and society. But to root out moral evil and sin, two things are necessary: turning away from sin and reconciliation.

Turning away from sin is called conversion (from the Latin word, *convertere*, meaning "to turn, to change, to go in an opposite direction"). It involves three processes: the recognition of the existence of sin of whatever kind; the admission of the act or state of sin; and the reconciliation of the person, or group, to the society from which a person or group is alienated. *This is the essence of the Sacrament of Reconciliation.*

6.3 What the Sacrament of Reconciliation Is

The Sacrament of Reconciliation is an act of the Church in which sins repented of and confessed to a proper minister are forgiven by the minister in the name of Jesus. The sacrament is a sign of conversion and reconciliation because the penitent turns away from his or her sins and becomes reconciled to God and the community through the actions of the minister.

The Sacrament of Reconciliation became a part of the Catholic sacramental liturgy to help people who had separated themselves from the community by extremely serious sins to reestablish their special relationship with God and be reconciled to the community of believers.*

After confessing their sin, or sins, to the bishop, they were received back into the community by the bishop in the name of Jesus. (When the number of believers became too great for the bishop to attend to personally, he delegated his forgiving powers to his ministers, the priests.)

---

*At first, denying the faith, murder, and adultery were the sins that separated a person from the believing community. Later, other serious sins which also attacked the essence and holiness of the community were added to the list that required reconciliation. (See 1 Corinthians 6:9–11.)

The matter of the Sacrament of Reconciliation is serious sin.* The form is the confessing and the forgiveness by the priest. Whatever form the ritual takes, it must signify conversion, repentance, and reconciliation. Many forms of the sacrament are in use in the Church today. The two most common are "private" (or individual) and community reconciliation.

The Sacrament of Reconciliation is a sacrament because it is a solemn, public, official act of the church signifying and affecting the conversion and reconciliation of a sinner. It is a celebration because the whole community of the

Church (in the person of a priest, a small group assembled officially, or a parish, a diocese, and so forth) welcomes the alienated person back into the community. It is an act of worship because through the sacrament a person acknowledges his failure to cooperate in God's plan for his destiny and his willingness to become reconciled to God and to the people of God.

The Church takes its cue for the Sacrament of Reconciliation from the biblical themes of God's mercy and willingness to forgive and from Jesus' own example of mercy and forgiveness. Both are vividly expressed in the famous parable of the Prodigal Son. It is in this parable that we see portrayed all the aspects of the Sacrament of Reconciliation: free choice to turn away from the Father; the sinful action; the recognition of the condition of sin; the resolution to

---

*Not-so-serious sins need not be confessed, though they may be. The common form of reconciliation for the common sins all Catholics commit is "The Penitential Rite" at the beginning of Mass.

turn away from sin and return to the Father; the act of returning and confession of guilt; the asking for forgiveness; the acceptance by the Father; the family celebration over the return of the one who went away. The parable is told in the Gospel according to Luke, chapter 15. It is one of several Luke gives to illustrate the nature of God's forgiveness.

There was a man who had two sons [Jesus said.] The younger one said to his father, "Father, give me now my share of the property." So the father divided the property between his two sons. After a few days the younger son sold his part of the property and left home with the money. He went to a country far away, where he wasted his money in reckless living. He spent everything he had. Then a severe famine spread over that country, and he was left without a thing. So he went to work for one of the citizens of that country, who sent him out to his farm to take care of the pigs. He wished he could fill himself with the bean pods the pigs ate, but no one gave him any. At last he came to his senses and said: "All my father's hired workers have more than they can eat, and here I am, about to starve! I will get up and go to my father and say, 'Father, I have sinned against God and against you. I am no longer fit to be called your son; treat me as one of your hired workers.' " So he got up and started back to his father.

He was still a long way from home when his father saw him; his heart was filled with pity and he ran, threw his arms around his son, and kissed him. "Father," the son said, "I have sinned against God and against you. I am no longer fit to be called your son." But the father called his servants: "Hurry!" he said. "Bring the best robe and put it on him. Put a ring on his finger and shoes on his feet. Then go get the prize calf and kill it, and let us celebrate with a feast! For this son of mine was dead, but now he is alive; he was lost, but now he has been found." And so the feasting began.

(Luke 15:11–24)

The Necessary Elements in the Sacrament of Reconciliation

There is an effect that often arises from the recognition of personal sin and from the confession of sins in the Sacrament of Reconciliation that we might call the "personal effect." That is, a person might so concentrate on the personal effects of sin or on personal guilt and personal forgiveness that he might ignore or forget about the social effects of sin and the importance of the reconciliatory aspects of the Sacrament of Reconciliation.

It is easy to see that the social effects of evil are far greater than the personal effects. Vote fraud, for example, or stealing welfare checks, or cheating at cards, or bribery, aggravated assault, perjury, slander, and the like, have consequences that reach farther and affect other people more deeply than they affect the individual sinner. Over and above that, biblical revelation and the early history of the Church demonstrate that the social effects of sin and the importance of reconciliation are far more important than the personal effects of sin. Israel's sins affected the welfare of the whole society of Israel. Turning to God and repenting of sin brought the whole nation back to God's favor, and Israel as a nation prospered. In the early Church sins that seriously affected society were considered most serious and most in need of forgiveness and reconciliation. These included, as we said, murder, which attacked and affected human society in general; adultery, which attacked and affected the family; and apostasy, which attacked and affected the Christian community. In light of this, it is important that more attention be paid to the reconciliation aspect of the sacrament than to the personal results—as important as these are.

Because it is a sacrament of the forgiveness of sin, and its purpose is conversion and reconciliation, everything that is done in the "Rite of Reconciliation" has these goals in mind. Whether it is individual or communal, the Sacrament of Reconciliation has these parts:

1. the recognition of sin and/or the state of sinfulness on the part of the individual

2. true sorrow for sins committed

3. the confession of sins

4. absolution by a priest

5. a positive expression in living of turning away from sin

Because of what it is, the Sacrament of Reconciliation should be received seriously. It is a personal encounter with a forgiving God, a positive sign of God's acceptance of our sorrow, and a means of grace to reform our lives. It is an act of the Church making it possible for a person to be at peace with himself, at peace with his believing community, and at peace with the world. Like all the sacraments it has both personal and social effects. It enables a person to be holy and in so doing makes the world a better place.

The Structure of the Communal Reception of The Sacrament of Reconciliation

1. **Introductory Rites**

   a. Song or recitation of psalm
   b. Greetings
   c. Opening comments
   d. Introductory prayer

2. **Celebration of the Word of God**

   a. Reading from Scripture
   b. Song or recitation of psalm
   c. Reading from the Gospel
   d. Homily
   e. Examination of conscience

3. **Rite of Reconciliation**

   a. General confession of sins
   b. Litany or hymn
   c. Lord's Prayer
   d. Concluding prayer
   e. Individual confession
      (1) advice or dialogue
      (2) discussion or penance-satisfaction
      (3) absolution
      (4) imposition of hands

4. **Proclamation of Praise**

   a. Invitation to offer thanks and praise
   b. Exhortation to good works
   c. Hymn, psalm recitation, or litany
   d. Group prayer of thanksgiving

5. **Concluding Rite**

   a. Blessing
   b. Dismissal

The Structure of the Sacrament of Reconciliation For Individuals

1. Preparation
2. Reception of the Penitent
3. Liturgy of the word
4. Confession of sins
5. Prayer of the penitent and absolution

A Short Rite for Individuals

1. Confession of sins
2. Acceptance of penance satisfaction
3. Invitation to contrition
4. Absolution
5. Dismissal

In your local newspaper, find examples of sins that adversely affect the world, our nation, or your area. Tell what the bad effects are.

What are the social effects of the following sins when they are committed by persons your age? Give examples.

unlawful use of drugs

vandalism

stealing

racial prejudice

cheating

lying

What sins besides "the big three" of the early Church would you consider extremely serious—enough to require reconciliation with the believing community? Explain your reasons.

On page 177 a sample of the rite for the Sacrament of Reconciliation is given. It is a rite used for the community celebration. Go over it carefully and be prepared to show how the necessary elements of the sacrament are present.

The Sacrament of Reconciliation (A Rite for Communal Reception)

1. INTRODUCTION

LEADER: Let us begin our celebration of this sacrament with a moment of silence during which we prepare ourselves for the sacrament we are going to receive.

Pause. A hymn may be sung or a psalm recited.

PRIEST: Father in heaven, we come together to confess our sins. We come with deep confidence that, as we prepare together, we will see more clearly your great concern for us, so that when we come to meet your Son in confession, we will be open to that meeting and will obtain forgiveness for our sins and strength to overcome evil through him whose love for us lasts forever.

PEOPLE: *Father, hear our prayer.*

2. CELEBRATION OF GOD'S WORD

Two or more selections from the Scripture may be read, but one of them must be from the gospels. If more than two selections are read, one of them may be from a source other than the Scripture.

After each of the readings which precede the reading of the gospel, the people ought to respond to the reading with an appropriate prayer or the recitation of a psalm similar in tone to the following:

PEOPLE:
*From the depths
I call to you, O Lord.
Lord, listen
to my cry for help!
Listen compassionately
to my pleading.
If you never overlooked
our sins, Lord,
Lord, could anyone survive?
But you do forgive us:
and for that we revere you.
I wait for the Lord,
my soul waits for him,
I rely on his promise,
my soul relies on the Lord
more than a watchman
on the coming of dawn.
Let us rely on the Lord
as much as the watchman on the dawn!
For it is with the Lord
that mercy is to be found,
and a generous redemption;
it is he who
redeems us from our sins.*
—Psalm 130

After the gospel selection is read by the priest, a homily (sermon) is given by the priest.

3. PREPARATION FOR CONFESSION

LEADER: Let us place ourselves in the presence of God and honestly and humbly open ourselves to His action. We know that by our sins we have hurt the members of the Christian community and contributed to sin in the world.

LIVE YOUR INDIVIDUALITY TO THE FULL

Let us spend a few moments examining ourselves: how we live, what our attitudes are, what are the customary ways in which we commit sin—maybe without even thinking about it.

The examination of conscience may be made in silence or helps may be read aloud by the priest or someone in the congregation. The following is an example of what may be done in silence or read aloud.

Have I placed things, or money, people or pleasure before my duty to God?

Have I been content with half-hearted participation in God's actions in my life?

Have I scandalized others by my words or my actions, not leading them as I should?

Have I taken people for granted, treating some with indifference, some with contempt?

Especially the members of my family?

Have I pursued my school work as I should?

Have I cheated or lied or given excuses about my work?

Have I tried to get even with others?

Do I have in thought, action or word the respect I should have for my sexual powers?

Do I respect the sexual powers of others?

Have I been guilty of stealing, or vandalism, or of carelessness with the property of others?

Is my word my bond, or do I lie or color the truth to meet my own selfish needs?

Do I drive safely or am I a show-off with the car?

Do I take proper care of my health?

Do I use my talents for the benefit of others or for my own selfish ends?

Have I been truly charitable?

Have I treated others than my friends the way a human being ought to be treated?

How do I really stand before God at this moment?

Am I self-satisfied, unconscious of my weakness and sins, or carefully blocking them out of my consciousness?

4. SACRAMENTAL CONFESSION

LEADER: For the reception of the sacrament you are asked to confess to one of the priests. It is suggested that you make your confession brief, covering one particular area of concern in your life. However, it is necessary to mention all serious sins. The priest will then give you absolution.

After all have been to confession, we will participate in a communal penance.

During the actual time of confessions, the group may listen to readings, meditate in silence, or participate in the recitation of psalms or prayers. When all have finished confessing, the community penance service begins.

5. COMMUNITY PENANCE PRAYER

PRIEST: O my God, I am sorry for having offended you. You know and understand that I sin out of human weakness. You know and understand also that in the deepest part of

myself, I do love you, or at least want to love you. You forgive me so easily, so willingly, yes, even so gladly. Please teach me to forgive myself. Teach me to be patient with myself, and help me to learn from my sin. Help me to learn how much I must depend on you, for the struggle against sin is never over until death. Help me to see that my love for you is, and will be, purified in this very struggle, that all growth and love is accompanied by suffering, disappointment and pain. And if I can come to see and accept myself as you see and accept me, then let me grow in knowledge, and love and acceptance of all the people in my life. Let me show them the forgiveness and love that you show me. I ask you these things in the name of your son and our brother, Jesus Christ.

ALL: *Amen.*

(The individual penance prescribed for each person ought to be taken care of by each person at his own convenience. The community act of sorrow does not replace the individual antidote for sin prescribed by the priest in the actual confession itself.)

6. CONCLUSION

PRIEST: Lord Jesus Christ, we thank you for standing in our midst this evening to bring us the gift of your peace. You have forgiven all our sins and now you send us forth as you sent your apostles, just as the Father sent you. We are strengthened by this trust and confidence but we know our weakness. Therefore we turn with You to the Father and pray as you have taught us:

PEOPLE: *Our Father.* . . .

PRIEST: Put on love and the peace of Christ will reign in your hearts. Be merciful and always be thankful. May the blessings of Almighty God, the Father, the Son, and the Holy Spirit be with you.

LEADER: Our closing hymn is. . . .

PRIEST: Go in the peace our Savior promised to all who love him.

PEOPLE: *Thanks be to God.*

Now that you have studied the theology of the Sacrament of Reconciliation and examined its structure and a suggested rite, discuss the theology and meaning of the sacrament with your classmates, using the following questions as a guide to the discussion.

What seems to be the basic difference between the Sacrament of Penance and asking God for forgiveness privately?

What do you understand as the important action of God in the Sacrament of Reconciliation?

What seems to be the "moment" of the sacrament?

Do you think that a person ought to go to confession even though he or she may not have any serious sins to confess? Why?

What do you understand by the term "conversion" as it is used in the Sacrament of Reconciliation?

Can you think of any way in which this sacrament is related to Baptism?

Can you suggest other areas of life where an act of conversion and reconciliation might prove useful? Explain.

6.4 The Anointing of the Sick

It is a safe bet that you have not received what is popularly called "The Sacrament of the Sick." It is also a rather safe bet that you have never seen the sacrament administered. You've all heard of it, but do you know what it is? Do you know how it is administered? Do you know who should receive it? Would you know what to do if someone in your family became suddenly seriously sick or if a friend of yours were critically injured in an accident? Would you call a priest immediately after calling for a doctor and an ambulance? Why, in fact, would you call a priest, if you even thought of it?

Catholics call a priest when someone they know is seriously sick so that the person may receive the sacrament designed to bring comfort, assurance, and healing to the sick person.

This sacrament of the sick, more properly called "The Anointing of the Sick," is a sacrament reserved for the very sick, for the elderly, and for those in danger of dying from injury or surgery. In the sacrament, the priest, or authorized minister, anoints the sick person with blessed oil and prays that God will cure, comfort, or heal the sick person.

The Sacrament of the Sick is not received very often, though the elderly may receive it many times. Oftentimes it is not received at all—when death is unexpected and swift. When it is received, it is a sign of comfort and a sign of hope.

The Anointing of the Sick is a sacrament of physical and spiritual healing. Christians have always believed that sickness is not limited to particular parts of the body. They have believed (and now modern medical science agrees) that illness affects the *whole* person—body and spirit. You, for example, might have a stomachache, but you feel bad "all over." Your spirits are down, your emotions are negative, and your mood is anything but happy.

So, the Church, in addressing itself to the needs of the sick and the elderly, addresses itself to the whole person—to the body and the spirit. If physical healing occurs, so much the better. Spiritual, emotional, and psychological healing always occur because the Anointing of the Sick is a *sacrament*. It is a personal encounter with Christ for the spiritual good of the person receiving it. It is for this reason that a person's family and friends should see to it that he receives the Sacrament when he is seriously sick. Through it, the person encounters Christ

in his healing, comforting, compassionate role as savior of the world.

The Anointing of the Sick has been an act of the Church from its very first days. The first communities of believers were very conscious of Jesus' own concern for and compassionate treatment of the sick and the suffering. Many had seen Jesus in action, and all had heard through the Gospel stories about how Jesus treated the lepers, the outcasts of society. They heard about his care for older people in pain and his sympathy for those who had experienced death in their loved ones.* It is no wonder that the same compassion, care, and treatment of those who needed Jesus' healing presence became a regular act of the Church. (See the Epistle of James 5:14, 15.)

---

*See the Gospel according to Luke, 5:12–17, 17:11–19; 7:11–17, 8:40–48, 13:10–13. See also the Gospel according to John 5:1–15 and 11:1–44.

6.5 The Effects of the Sacrament

The seriously sick and elderly need care, comfort, and assurance. They need to know that someone cares. When the priest, or authorized minister of the Church, comes, the sick and elderly know that God cares and the Church cares.

When the priest, or authorized minister, acting as the official minister of the Church, comes to administer the sacrament of The Anointing of the Sick, he brings Christ's own comfort, care, and hope to the person receiving the sacrament. He counsels, prays with, and prays for the sick or elderly person. He places his hands on the sick person, anoints the forehead and hands with the blessed oil, and says: "Through this holy anointing and his great kindness, may the Lord fill you with the power of His Holy Spirit. In His goodness may He ease your suffering and extend His saving grace to you, freed from all the power of sin."*

Through the words and actions of the priest, the special grace of the sacrament is signified and conferred. The special help of God for the sick person becomes present. Through this sacrament, the sick receive strength in suffering, forgiveness of sins, and peace of mind.

The Anointing of the Sick, however, is not only a sign of Christ acting to soothe, comfort, and heal the sick. It is also a

---

*What is said is used when the sacrament is administered to many people at a time also. The sacrament may be given to groups in a hospital setting or in a church. When it is administered in a church, it is often a part of the Mass.

sign of hope. It is an assurance that the special relationship with God which Catholics believe they experience is firm, lasting, and eternal. For those who are dying, it is a further sign of hope. It is a sign of Christ preparing his people for their life with God after earthly death. It is a sign that death is not to be feared as the end of life. It is to be looked on as a prelude to eternal life when people will share the life of God in their own risen dimension of existence.

Christians believe that just as Jesus rose from the dead and now lives his Risen Life, they, too, will rise to a new life in Christ when they have finished their limited life here on earth. For this reason, the Anointing of the Sick is not only a comfort for the sick and the elderly; it is a sign of hope for the living.

On the following pages is The Rite of Anointing of the Sick. Go over it carefully; then answer the questions below on another sheet of paper.

Why is the Christian belief in life after death a source of comfort to the seriously sick and the dying?

In what way is the Sacrament of the Anointing of the Sick a sign of Christ acting here and now?

Why do you think your book calls the Sacrament of the Sick a sign of comfort and a sign of hope?

Can you see any relationship between this sacrament and the Sacrament of Baptism?

You hear some Catholics say that you should not "call the priest" until the last minute. Can you give any reason why this is not the right view of the nature of this sacrament?

Why are the matter and form of the sacrament appropriate to the purpose of the sacrament?

The Rite of Anointing of the Sick

1. PREPARATION FOR THE CELEBRATION

Before he anoints a sick person, the priest should inquire about his condition in order to plan the celebration properly and to choose the biblical readings and the prayers. If possible he should make this preparation with the sick person or his family, while explaining to them the significance of the sacrament.

If the sick person is not confined to bed, he may receive the sacrament of anointing in the church or some other fitting place, where there is a suitable chair or place prepared for him and enough room for his relatives and friends to take part.

The rite described below may also be used for anointing several sick persons at the same time. In this case, the priest lays hands on each person individually and anoints each one, using the appointed form. Everything else is done once for all, and the remaining prayers are recited in the plural.

2. RITE FOR ANOINTING

Wearing the vestments proper to this ministry, the priest greets the sick person and others who are present in a friendly manner.

He may use this greeting: Peace to this house and to all who live within it!

or: The peace of the Lord be with you always.

(In hospitals the priest should consider the other sick people: whether they should be included in the celebration or, if they are not Christians, whether they might be offended.)

If it is the custom, the priest sprinkles the sick person and the room with holy water, saying:

PRIEST: Cleanse me, Lord, from all my sins; wash me, and I shall be whiter than snow. (or: wash away my iniquity.)

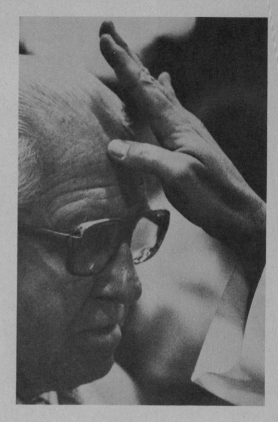

Then he addresses those present using these or similar words.

PRIEST: Dear brothers and sisters.*
We have come together in the name of our Lord Jesus Christ, who restored the sick to health, and who himself suffered so much for our sake. He is present among us as we recall the words of the apostle James: "Is there anyone sick among you? Let him call for the elders of the Church, and let them pray over him and anoint him in the name of the Lord. This prayer, made in faith, will save the sick man. The Lord will restore his health, and if he has committed any sins, they will be forgiven." Let us entrust our sick brother (sister) to the power and strength of Jesus Christ, that Christ may ease his (her) sufferings and restore his (her) health.

---

*At the discretion of the priest, other words which seem more suitable under the circumstances such as *friends, dearly beloved, brethren,* may be used. This also applies to parallel instances in the liturgy.

The priest may begin the penitential rite either here or after the reading:

PRIEST: My brothers and sisters, to prepare ourselves to celebrate this holy anointing, let us call to mind our sins.

The penitential rite follows according to one of the forms found in the Order of Mass. Then a brief text from scripture is read by the priest or some other person. Then the priest reads a selection from the Gospel, for example, Matthew 8:5–10, 13. He may then give a brief commentary on the reading.

The following litany may be used either here, after the anointing or, according to circumstances, at some other point. The priest may adapt or shorten the text as needed.

PRIEST: My brothers and sisters, with faith let us ask the Lord to hear our prayers for N., our brother (sister). Lord, through this holy anointing, come to him (her) with love and mercy.

RESPONSE: *Lord, hear our prayer.*

PRIEST: Free him (her) from all harm.

RESPONSE: *Lord, hear our prayer.*

PRIEST: Give life and health to our brother (sister), on whom we lay our hands in your name.

RESPONSE: *Lord, hear our prayer.*

PRIEST: Relieve the sufferings of all the sick [here present].

RESPONSE: *Lord, hear our prayer.*

PRIEST: Assist all those dedicated to the care of the sick.

RESPONSE: *Lord, hear our prayer.*

PRIEST: Lamb of God, you take away the sins of the world.

RESPONSE: *Have mercy on us.*

(Other forms may be used.)

The priest then lays his hands on the head of the sick person in silence.

If oil is to be blessed during the rite, he says the following prayer.

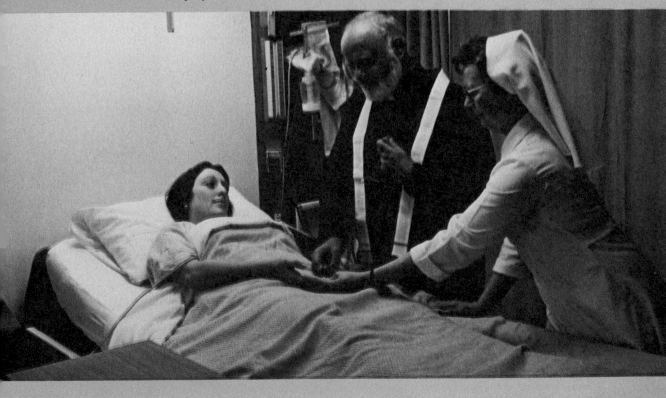

PRIEST: Let us pray.

Lord God, Father of all comfort, it was your
will to restore health to the sick through
your Son, Jesus Christ.
Mercifully listen to the prayer we make in faith
for those who believe in you, on whom the
elders of the Church have placed their hands,
and who will be anointed in your name:
May they receive the health you offer in this
sacrament.

Send your Holy Spirit, the Consoler, from
heaven to bless this oil, a work of nature, an
ointment to strengthen the body.
May all who are anointed with this oil be freed
from every pain, illness, and disease, and be
made well again in body, mind, and soul.

Father, may this oil, which you have blessed for
our use produce its healing effect in the
name of our Lord Jesus Christ, who lives and
reigns with you for ever and ever.

RESPONSE: *Amen.*

Then the priest takes the oil and anoints the
sick person on the forehead and the hands,
saying:

PRIEST: Through this holy anointing and his
great love for you, may the Lord fill you with
the power of his Holy Spirit.

RESPONSE: *Amen.*

PRIEST: In his goodness may he ease your
suffering and extend his saving grace to you,
freed from all the power of sin.

RESPONSE: *Amen.*

Afterwards the priest says the prayer which
is best suited to the sick person's condition, and
the rite concludes with the Lord's Prayer recited
by all and the blessing.

PRIEST: May God the Father bless you.

RESPONSE: *Amen.*

PRIEST: May God the Son make you well
again.

RESPONSE: *Amen.*

PRIEST: May God the Holy Spirit fill you with
his radiant light.

RESPONSE: *Amen.*

PRIEST: May God protect your body from
harm, and grant health to your soul.

RESPONSE: *Amen.*

PRIEST: May he shine on your heart, and lead
you to eternal life.

RESPONSE: *Amen.*

PRIEST: (And may almighty God, the Father,
and the Son, and the Holy Spirit, bless you all.)

RESPONSE: *Amen.*

(If the sick person is to receive communion,
this takes place after the Lord's Prayer and
according to the Rite of Communion of the
Sick.)

Conclusion

The Catholic Church, acting as Christ in society, addresses itself to the real needs of its people. It brings them into "the new people of God" in Baptism and invokes the presence of the Spirit in Confirmation. It reunites them in peace in the Sacrament of Reconciliation and enables them to partake of spiritual food in the Eucharist. It provides them with special ministers in the Sacrament of Orders and sacramentalizes their love in Matrimony. It comforts them when they are seriously sick by the Anointing of the Sick.

Through its healing sacraments, the Church cares for its most needy members. It calls to them, embraces them, heals them, and brings them to the Father just as Jesus did. It is for them, too, that Jesus asked his followers to carry on his work. They have done so, making Christ present to all who seek him out.

Summary

The world is an imperfect, sinful place in need of redemption.

Christ has given the means for this redemption in the lives of his people, the Church. He has given them his healing sacraments to reinforce or reestablish, if necessary, their special relationship with God.

The Sacrament of Reconciliation provides the means for the forgiveness of sins.

The Anointing of the Sick provides healing, comfort, and hope to those who are seriously sick or in danger of dying.

Words You Should Know

Be sure that you can define the words given below. If there are any you are not sure of, look them up in the Word List on page 234.

adversely	global	reconciliation
anoint	leper	shoddy
catechism	penitent	vandalism
compassionate	plaguing	wary
context	prelude	

For Review, Discussion, Research, and Reflection

1. Explain how the Gospels show that Jesus had power over evil.

2. What definition is given for sin in your book? Be able to explain what it means.

3. Discuss the kinds of sin and the degrees of sin as these are described in your book. What does your book mean by "the habit of sin"?

4. Why does your book suggest that the social effects of sin are more serious than the personal effects? Do you think they are? Why? Why not?

5. What is "conversion"? Why does conversion involve three processes?

6. What is "The Sacrament of Reconciliation"? Why is it an important sacrament of the Catholic Church? What are its basic elements? What are its "action," "grace," and "continuity"?

7. What is "The Sacrament of the Sick"? Why is it called "a healing sacrament"? What are its "action," "grace," and "continuity"?

8. Why is life after death an essential aspect of Christian faith?

9. In an open forum, discuss why people fear death, and whether Christians should fear it.

10. Conduct an informal survey among your friends about their belief in life after death. Do the same among adults you know. In each case, try to find out why they believe as they do. Report your findings to the class.

11. In an open forum, discuss what life after death may be like. Look up 1 Corinthians 2:9 to see what St. Paul said.

12. Read Revelation 21. Be prepared to discuss what it says in symbols as these relate to what we believe about life after death.

13. Reread the quotation that introduces this chapter. Reflect on its meaning for you personally. Do you think it would make a good prayer for a person when a close friend or relative is sick?

14. During one of your "moments of prayer," pray for the abandoned sick of the world.

15. Prepare a few thoughts concerning a rite for reconciliation that you can share with your class in preparation for a class liturgy of reconciliation.

Experiencing a Special Relationship with God: Matrimony and Orders

What is man that you should be
  mindful of him,
    or the son of man that you
    should care for him?
You have made him little less
  than the angels,
    and crowned him with glory
    and honor.
You have given him rule over the
  works of your hands,
    putting all things under his
    feet:
All sheep and oxen,
  yes, and the beasts of the field,
The birds of the air, the fishes of
  the sea,
    and whatever swims the paths
    of the seas.
O Lord, our Lord,
  how glorious is your name over
  all the earth!

—Psalm 8:5–10

7.1 People Are Created in God's Image

Most people take the fact of their life and their humanity for granted. They rarely think of the complicated interplay of the various human forces that make them what they are.

How, for example, does your mind work? How is it that you can read the ink spots that make up the printing on this page? Why do you remember things? How can you look forward to next year? Why are you *you* and not someone else? As a matter of fact, what are you anyway?

Our religious community thinks it has an answer for those complicated questions. For us, the answer lies in our sacred literature, the Bible.

Creation of Adam—from the Sistine Chapel by Michelangelo

"In the beginning," goes the first verse of Genesis, the first book of our Bible, ". . . God created the heavens and the earth." It is fitting, of course, that the Bible should begin at the beginning! But there is more to this first chapter of Genesis than the story of the origins of the world as the ancient Israelites pictured it.

The Book of Genesis says more than "God created the heavens and the earth." It tells people of their role in God's creative plans. "Be fertile and multiply," Genesis has God saying to people. "Fill the earth and subdue it," He says. God does not say to other creatures, "subdue the earth" (that is, bring the earth under some kind of control). He says it only to people. Why?

Genesis has God saying this only to people because only people are made, as Genesis says, in the image of God. "Let us make man in our image, after our likeness," verse 26 says. Verse 27 then says, "God created man in his image; in the divine image he created him."

What is this image, this likeness of God that makes people so different from all other living creatures? It is their ability to create. Other living things are able to reproduce. Only people are able to create. Only people are able to imagine, to plan, to devise means, and to make things better.

Although we generally think of creativity in terms of the great achievements in art, literature, architecture, music, and the like, creativity is within the capability of all human beings. Everyone can bring into being that which did not exist before. That is the nature of creativity.

To create a new human life and to bring people together in worship to celebrate life are two of the greatest human creations. In each, we are most like God: we create, with Him, new human beings, and we bring them into a life-sharing experience. It is these that the Church celebrates in its **Sacrament of Matrimony** and **Sacrament of Orders.** In them, the Church sacramentalizes God's creative gift to people.

Matrimony and Orders are special sacraments. They are reserved for a special life-style, a particular social function, and an exclusive purpose. They signify and cause a special action of God, a special grace, and a special kind of relationship with God.

The other sacraments are what we might call "general" sacraments. All who are baptized, for example, experience the same relationship with God that Baptism brings. The same Spirit energizes all who are confirmed. Christ is present in the same way to all in the Eucharist, and God's forgiveness embraces all who receive the Sacrament of Reconciliation.

Only those who are married, however, experience the special relationship with God and the special graces that are consequences of the Sacrament of Matrimony. They are reserved only for married couples. And only the ordained can receive the special graces of ordination and experience the special relationship with God that His special ministers do. They are reserved for those in Orders only.

7.2 The Sacrament of Matrimony: Sign of Love— Sign of Life

Another thing that many young people take for granted is their family. They take their parents, their home, their food, their clothing, their recreation—everything they have and are as a matter of course.

They see boys and girls going with each other, holding hands, hugging, and kissing. They know that many of them are

"making out" without any thought about what all these actions are and mean. The feelings they experience and the things they do are new and they are pleasurable. For many of them, that's all that counts. They don't relate the actions of sex with family. They "know" they'll get married some day, but they haven't the slightest idea of what marriage really is or what it means to raise a family.

And, exposed as they are to a variety of conflicting views of marriage, many young Catholics are unsure of their Church's view of marriage, of sex, of children, and of divorce. They don't understand the difference between what is called a "Christian" marriage and one that is not. To them, they both look the same.

On the surface, they do look alike, but in reality they are different. For Catholics, living in marriage is a religious act. For them, marriage is a sacrament. It is a religious act and a sacrament because it is considered within the total picture of the Christian way of life.

In the Catholic Church, marriage is not simply an important and intimate way of expressing a special kind of relationship with a person of the opposite sex. It is not only the living together of persons of the opposite sex, or a way of establishing a new family unit in society. Nor is it simply a way to perpetuate the human race through a life-style best suited for raising children. *In the Church, marriage is a way of living the faith.* In it, two Christians express who they are and what they are: Christians living together in love in response to the Christian view of life as life is experienced in Christian marriage.

In the Catholic Church, also, marriage is a sacrament, not because the Church says it is, or because, for Catholics, a priest is present and it is celebrated with religious ceremonies. It is a sacrament because it is a way of life in which God is present in a special way in the lives of the two baptized persons joined in Christ in a union of love. **It is a personal encounter with Christ by two baptized persons who live together as husband and wife in the social institution we call marriage.** It is an act of the Church which signifies and causes God's special graces and special relationship to become active in the lives of two Christians who commit themselves to a union called marriage.

> JUST AS BY BAPTISM CHRISTIANS ENTER INTO AND PARTICIPATE IN THE MYSTERY OF THE REDEMPTION, SO ALSO BY MARRIAGE CHRISTIANS ENTER INTO AND PARTICIPATE IN THE MYSTERY OF UNION WITH CHRIST.
>
> JOSEPH MARTOS

7.3 What Christian Marriage Is

In the eyes of Catholics, Christian marriage is special and sacred. It is special because it is living with a person of the opposite sex in an intimate and very personal way, not simply in response to biological, psychological, or cultural forces. It is living with a person of the opposite sex in an intimate and personal way in response to God's purpose in creating people of the opposite sex.

Then the Lord God said, "It is not good for the man to live alone. I will make a suitable companion to help him." . . . He formed a woman out of the rib and brought her to him. Then the man said, "At last, here is one of my own kind—Bone taken from my bone, and flesh from my flesh. 'Woman' is her name because she was taken out of man."

That is why a man leaves his father and mother and is united with his wife, and they become one. (Genesis 2:18, 22–24)

It is sacred because it is a sacrament. It is a sign of God's special saving activity in the lives of the two who are living as husband and wife in marriage. It is a sign of God's commitment of grace in the lives of the two people expressing their Christianity in marriage. It is a sign of the sacred love for each other that the man and the woman have. It is a sign of the cooperation of the husband and wife in the creative activity of God. It is the symbol of the union between Christ and his Church. (See the Epistle of St. Paul to the Ephesians 5:25–33.)

For Catholics, marriage is not simply two people who love each other sharing intimately their hopes and their lives. It is two people who love each other and share intimately their hopes and their lives together as Christians. It is the living together of two people who experienced the same divine relationship given by God in Baptism and who now share a special divine relationship because they are married.

For Catholics, marriage is also a sharing of body, mind, resources, grace, and faith in love. It is a relationship that transcends the human and incorporates the divine. It is the commitment to the sacredness of what Christians mean by marriage.

Two people live together in that special form of relationship-commitment because they love each other. People do get married, it is true, for other reasons, some of which are good and some not so good. But for the most part, in a relatively free society, people come together in marriage in response to their feelings for each other. Something happens between them: their body chemistry sets up a response in them that is unique and special. But such a response is more than an urge for physical release. It is an urge to share all that one has and is in a unique relationship that one has with no one else. When this relationship is pledged and carried out, it is called marriage. It is this that the Church sacramentalizes in the Sacrament of Matrimony.

What do you understand by the idea that you are created in God's image?

Discuss why Matrimony and Orders are called "special" sacraments.

What does your book mean by "taking life for granted"? Do you think most teenagers take their family and their family life for granted? Explain.

Discuss the difference between a marriage between two Catholics and one between two non-Christians.

Why do Catholics consider marriage a sacrament? Why do they think of it as special and sacred? Does TV present marriage as something special and sacred most of the time? Why? Why not?

7.4 Why Some Marriages Fail

No one can deny that marriage as an institution is in difficulty in certain parts of society. It does no good to say that even though one-third of the marriages in the United States end in divorce, two-thirds of the marriages entered into are happy and successful, or relatively so. The fact is that one marriage that ends up in divorce is too many because marriage, entered into in love and with high hopes, should be a source of happiness and fulfillment. In too many cases it is not. There are many reasons why this is so, not the least of which is, of course, the limitations of everyone's human existence. But over and above that, there are many economic, sociological, cultural, and personal reasons that work against many marriages being successful.

There is no question that arguments over money or about how it is to be used create serious problems for marriages, but poverty or money difficulties are not enough to cause most marriages to fail. It is also true that many men have a macho attitude which creates serious problems in marriage in the United States, especially. Lack of self-esteem and women's low status in some societies make marriage difficult at best. But by far the most serious reasons for marriage failures are the personal problems that pit two people against each other as adversaries. Among the many personal problems that cause marriages to fail are the following:

1. entering marriage for the wrong reasons,

2. expecting too much of marriage or of one's marriage partner,

3. considering marriage to be a continued romance expressed in intense feelings and expressions of love,

4. placing selfish concerns first,

5. rejecting personal self-discipline,

6. giving in to bodily desires in excessive drinking of alcoholic beverages, the use of harmful drugs, and sexual intimacies with other persons,

7. physical brutality, psychological abuse, and using foul, vulgar, and degrading language in speaking to or about one's marriage partner,

8. severely distasteful personal habits in eating, dressing, cleanliness, manners, and speaking

One of the most serious threats to marriage in this modern age, however, is a lack of a firm commitment to marriage as a way of life or to marriage as a permanent way of life. Such a lack of commitment is expressed in such spoken or

unspoken expressions as "why get married," "until our love dies," "if it works out," and the like. This lack of commitment creates a condition or stipulation that destroys full trust or puts doubts in the mind. Both are enemies of true love, the one necessary ingredient of happy marriages.

In an open forum discuss why personal problems and habits create conditions making some marriages fail. Give examples without mentioning any names.

Consult Ann Landers, Dear Abby, or other such materials over a three-day period. Make a list of the problems people present regarding marriage or their love life.

Discuss why a lack of commitment is psychologically unsound for a happy marriage.

Why do you think that society advises against teenage marriages? Why, then, are there so many teens marrying?

7.5 The Catholic Church's Concern in Catholic Marriages

It is because of these problems and challenges that two people might experience in living together, and because marriage is a sacrament, that the Church expresses great concern about marriage. It insists that Catholics understand its nature when they contemplate marriage in the Church.

Because of long experience, the Church is very practical when the question of marriage comes up. While preaching the divine sacredness of marriage and upholding the Christian ideal of marriage, the Church also presents guidelines and safeguards for its people in this the most volatile and fragile of human relationships. It does so, not simply to protect marriage as a social institution and sacramental reality, but also to help its people contemplating marriage to enter it with an informed mind as well as a loving heart. That is why the Church is so insistent on the life-long commitment in marriage and is reluctant to recognize divorce. That is why the Church teaches openness to having children and decries abortion. That is why the Church teaches that intimate sexual actions between two people who are not married to each other are sinful.

This teaching creates difficulty for unmarried people experiencing the full force of their sexual urges. They look upon the intimate expression of sexual

response to be natural—which it is. The body, after all, responds to things which excite it sexually. It is not the feeling that is wrong. It is what a person does in response to the feeling that determines its rightness or wrongness. And that is what the Church is concerned about.

The Church, you see, understands that intimate sexual actions are natural—and urgent. It also understands the delicate interplay of the psychological forces at work in sexual intimacies and what intimate sexual actions mean. It knows that sexual intimacies cannot be separated from their meaning and purpose. *That is why the Church teaches that intimate sexual actions, and especially sexual intercourse, must be considered in the total context of their own meaning and their meaning in Christian marriage.*

For Christians, sexual intercourse is not simply an extremely pleasurable bodily act. It is a bodily act with deep spiritual and creative meaning. It is not simply a sign of total giving and total receiving. It is also a sign of total love, and the means for creating new life in Christ. **For Christians, sexual intercourse is a holy action with deep personal, social, and sacramental meaning. It is a sign of love and a sign of life.**

If sexual intercourse and the intimate sexual actions leading up to sexual intercourse, are understood in this light, it is easy to see why the Church teaches that, for its members, sexual intimacies should be expressed in a truly loving, creative, and sacramental situation—that is, in marriage.

7.6 All Actions in Marriage Are Sacramental

As we have said, in the Catholic Church, living in marriage is a sacrament. It is a sign of God's creative activity in the lives of the two married partners. The wedding ceremony is the public ratification of the expressed intent of two people to live together in that special way of life we call marriage.

Like any sacrament, matrimony has signs and symbols which signify and are the marriage reality. The mutual giving and receiving of the free intention of the two parties to live together in marriage, signified by the spoken words of giving and receiving, constitute the "moment" of the sacrament. From that moment on, the two people are "one body in Christ." From that moment on, they participate together in the special action of God in their married lives. Their living together in mutual love is the sign of their living the Sacrament of Marriage. Because living in marriage is sacramental, every action of the two parties done in love is sacramental. These are not only the so-called small actions, such as doing the dishes or going to work. They are also the major actions such as caring for a child, tending a sick partner, making great sacrifices for the good of the family, showing signs of affection, or making love.

There are, of course, other sacramental signs and symbols in the wedding ceremony and in married life that also signify the sacrament of married life. The exchange of rings (or whatever else is symbolic in a particular culture), the wearing of the wedding rings throughout the marriage, the sharing of goods and burdens, doing things together, mutual fidelity, and the like, are all signs of living the Sacrament of Matrimony.

The presence of the priest who initiates the moment of the sacrament, receives the intention of the couple in the name of the Church, and blesses the couple in the name of the Church is a sign that the marriage is an official, public act of worship of the Church. The presence of witnesses who represent the entire Christian community, and the celebration of the wedding by friends are signs of the Christian community's participation in the joy of expressed love and the acceptance of the married couple as a new family unit in the Christian community. The celebration of the wedding ceremony itself as an act of religion is a sign of the holiness and sacredness of marriage in the Christian community.

It must not be forgotten, also, that the wedding ceremony and the living together in marriage are signs of God's immediate and continued activity (the special grace of the Sacrament of Matrimony) in the love relationship of married persons. God not only makes it possible for the marrying persons to love each other and to participate in His creative act, He also makes it possible for them to grow in married love through His special help when their lives are lived in love. It is for this reason that Catholic Christians involve themselves in the sacramental aspects of marriage, fulfilling the requirements of the sacrament to make their marriage a true sign of love and life.

It is because marriage is a sign of love, and because marriage provides the societal situation that is best for bringing children into the world and raising them in the Christian life that the Sacrament of Matrimony is called "a creation sacrament." More than any other, perhaps, it shows how people reflect God's image: through their ability to create new life in love.

Answer the following questions on another sheet of paper. Be prepared to discuss your answers with the members of your class.

Your book says that living in marriage for Christians is a religious act. What does it mean by "a religious act"?

Discuss why marriage is a sacrament in the Catholic Church.

Many people think of the Sacrament of Matrimony only in terms of the wedding ceremony. What does your book suggest is a wider understanding of the sacrament?

What is the "moment" of the Sacrament of Matrimony? In "The Rite of Matrimony" (page 204) this moment is given. Quote the words which indicate this moment.

Why does your book call The Sacrament of Matrimony a sign of love and a sign of life?

Read what the priest says in Part III of "A Wedding Ceremony." Reflect on its meaning in the love relationship of marriage.

Discuss why Catholic Christians should be married, as they say, "in the Church."

Discuss why your book implies that living in marriage is the most fragile and volatile of human relationships.

Why does the Catholic Church consider sexual intercourse before marriage to be sinful? In the view of the Church what is sexual intercourse a sign of?

What does Joseph Martos say about the importance of the wedding ceremony?

However the value and meaning
of Christian marriage are understood,
the wedding ceremony is always an
important and meaningful occasion. Its
words and gestures, even the bearing
and expression of its participants,
symbolize to the bride and groom and
the others who are present the meaning
and importance of what is happening
and what is about to happen to this
couple. They are being transformed, and
they are going to be transformed even
further. And the wedding is a door
through which they enter into that
sacred transformation.

Joseph Martos
"Doors to the Sacred"

The Rite of Matrimony (Outside of Mass)

1. INTRODUCTORY RITE*

The bride and groom, their witnesses, and friends come together with the priest who says:
"We are gathered here together as Christ's people to witness the marriage of N. and N.

2. LITURGY OF THE WORD

One or two selections from Scripture are read, after which the priest speaks of the biblical meaning of marriage.

3. THE RITE OF MARRIAGE

The priest, addressing the bride and groom, says:

PRIEST: My dear friends, you have come together in the Church so that the Lord may seal and strengthen your love in the presence of the church's minister and this community. Christ abundantly blesses this love. He has already consecrated you in baptism and now he enriches and strengthens you by a special sacrament so that you may assume the duties of marriage in mutual and lasting fidelity. And so, in the presence of the Church, I ask you to state your intentions.

N. and N. have you come here freely and without reservation to give yourselves to each other in marriage?

(They responded separately in an appropriate way.)

PRIEST: Will you love and honor each other as man and wife for the rest of your lives?

(They responded separately in an appropriate way.)

PRIEST: Will you accept children lovingly from God, and bring them up according to the law of Christ and his Church?

(They responded separately in an appropriate way.)

The priest then invites the couple to declare their consent:

Since it is your intention to enter into marriage, join your right hands, and declare your consent before God and His Church.

*Although the wedding ceremony need not take place during Mass, it ordinarily does because marriage is, perhaps more than any other sacrament, a community or community-vocation sacrament. People marry not simply for themselves, but also for the life of the community whose continuity they make possible by their family-life situation. When the wedding ceremony takes place during Mass, the worshipping community is present and celebrates the community-life aspect of marriage in the community's most important community action, the celebration of the Eucharist. When the wedding ceremony takes place within the Mass, all parts of the Mass are directed to the sacramental aspects of marriage.

GROOM: N., I take you for my lawful wife, to have and to hold, from this day forward, for better, for worse, for richer, for poorer, in sickness and in health, until death parts us.

BRIDE: N., I take you for my lawful husband, to have and to hold, from this day forward, for better, for worse, for richer, for poorer, in sickness and in health, until death parts us.

Receiving their consent in the name of the entire Catholic Church, the priest says:

PRIEST: You have declared your consent to be husband and wife in the true sense of the term before the Church. May the Lord in his goodness strengthen your consent and fill you with all his blessings. In the name of the Church, I declare you man and wife. What God has joined, men must not divide.

All present responded as witnesses to the marriage:

Amen. God so wills it.

The priest, blessing the wedding rings says:

PRIEST: May the Lord bless these rings which you give to each other as a sign of your love and fidelity.

The bride and groom then respond appropriately.

GROOM: N., I place this ring on your finger as a sign that you are forever my wife.

BRIDE: N., here is my symbolic gift of love to you. Wear it in good health, in good faith, and in good love. You are my husband forever.

4. THE NUPTIAL BLESSING

The priest, facing the bride and bridegroom, with hands joined, says:

My dear friends, let us turn to the Lord and pray that he will bless with grace (N.), now married in Christ to (N.), and that he will unite in love the couple he has joined in this holy bond.

All pray silently for a short while. Then the priest extends his hands and continues:

Father, by your power you have made everything out of nothing.
In the beginning you created the universe and made mankind in your own likeness.
You gave man the constant help of woman so that man and woman should no longer be two, but one flesh, and you teach us that what you have united may never be divided.
Father, you have made the union of man and wife so holy a mystery that it symbolizes the marriage of Christ and his Church.
Father, by your plan man and woman are united, and married life has been established as the one blessing that was not forfeited by original sin or washed away in the flood.
Look with love upon this woman, your daughter, now joined to her husband in marriage.
She asks your blessing. Give her the grace of love and peace.

May she always follow the example of the holy women whose praises are sung in the scriptures.
May her husband put his trust in her and recognize that she is his equal and the heir with him to the life of grace.
May he always honor her and love her as Christ loves his bride, the Church.
Father, keep them always true to your commandments.
Keep them faithful in marriage and let them be living examples of Christian life.
Give them the strength which comes from the gospel so that they may be witnesses of Christ to others.
Bless them with children and help them to be good parents.
May they live to see their children's children.
And, after a happy old age, grant them fullness of life with the saints in the kingdom of heaven.
We ask this through Christ our Lord.

PEOPLE: *Amen.*

5. THE CONCLUSION

The priest then blesses the bride and groom.

PRIEST: May almighty God, with his Word of blessing, unite your hearts in the never-ending bond of pure love.

PEOPLE: *Amen.*

PRIEST: May your children bring you happiness, and may your generous love for them be returned to you, many times over.

PEOPLE: *Amen.*

PRIEST: May the peace of Christ live always in your hearts and in your home. May you have true friends to stand by you, both in joy and in sorrow. May you be ready and willing to help and comfort all who come to you in need. And may the blessings promised to the compassionate be yours in abundance.

PEOPLE: *Amen.*

7.7 The Sacrament of Orders: A Sign of Sacramental Ministry

THE FAMILY CIRCUS,
Reprinted courtesy The Register and Tribune Syndicate, Inc.

"Mommy, God's here!"

Almost every young Catholic at one time or another has had an idea of being a priest. Priests are generally admired, imitated, and sought after by Catholics, and are given a special kind of respect. They occupy a place of honor in the Catholic Church because of what they are and what they represent.

Every religion has what Catholics call priests—persons who act as official or semi-official contact persons with whatever is divine for a particular religion. Protestants have their ministers, Jews have their rabbis, Hindus have their gurus, Moslems have their imams, primitive religions have their witch doctors, and so forth. Even the religions people usually look on with suspicion have their "priests": sorcerers, witches, diviners, demon leaders, and the like.

What is unique about Catholicism, however, is that all Catholics believe that they share in the priesthood of Christ. "You, however, are a chosen race, a royal priesthood, a holy nation, a people he claims for his own to proclaim the glorious works of the One who called you from darkness into his marvelous light," St. Peter told his converts. (See 1 Peter 2:9.) Therefore, Catholics believe that they are called to do what Jesus did: honor the Father in prayer and worship and help establish the kingdom of God on earth.

Every aspect of Jesus' life was mission oriented. He preached, he taught, and he admonished. He comforted the poor, healed the sick, and embraced those who were alienated or outcasts of society. He prayed and taught others how to pray. He gave signs of his coming from God and acting for God among people. He established a new covenant in his body and blood through which he gave his followers a new form of worship and a means of unity. In other words, Jesus fulfilled the function of priest: he represented the people before God and God before the people.

Just as Jesus performed many functions in his role as priest, so do Christians perform many functions in their role as priests. All pray and some preach the word of God. Some teach, some care for the sick, the poor, and the alienated. Some fulfill the sacramental ministry of

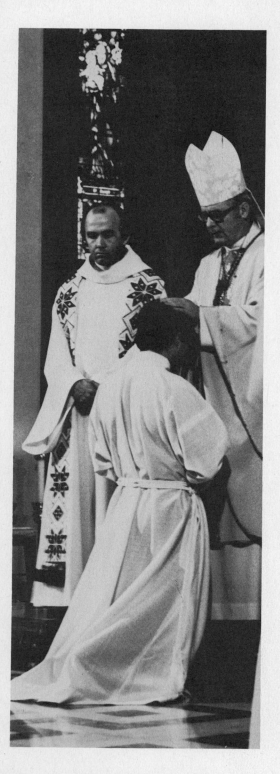

Jesus by administering the sacraments and offering the Eucharist. Those who fulfill the special sacramental ministry of Christ on earth are called priests.*

Although priests are active in all forms of the ministry, their special and particular ministry is to preside at the Eucharist, to be the agent (or sign) of God's activity in the sacramental life of the Church, and to preach the Gospel as helpers of the bishops in the ministry of the Church. It is for this that they are called by God and ordained by the Church. It is because of this that the ordination of persons for the priesthood is a sacrament. It is a sign to the believing community that the ordained person is the special representative of the community in the Eucharistic celebration, in the administration of the sacraments, and in preaching the word of God. Through it, the ordained person receives the special graces of God for his sacramental ministry. Through it, also, the ordained person experiences a special relationship with God.

The "moment" of the sacrament is the placing of the hands of the bishop on the head of the one being ordained and the vocalizing of the prayer of consecration (these are two separate acts). The prayer includes the following formula: "We ask you, all powerful Father, give this servant of yours the dignity of the presbyterate [priesthood]. Renew the Spirit of

*There are three "orders" or degrees of priestly ministry in the Catholic Church. The bishop is "chief" priest, or the pastor of all Catholics in his diocese. The pastor and the priests of each parish are the chief ministers of the sacraments for all Catholics in their parish. Deacons, the order below priests in function, are ordained to help the parish priests administer the sacraments and care for the affairs of the parish.

holiness within him. By your divine gift may he attain the second order in the hierarchy and exemplify right conduct in his life." Other symbolic actions are performed in the ceremony as signs to the community of the special ministry of priests, but these are symbolic only. They are not necessary to the completion of the sacramental moment.

Ordination, like all other sacraments, is a public action of the worshipping Church. It takes place, ideally, in the presence of the believing community (at Sunday Mass, for example) who acknowledge their assent to the ordination by responding to the public prayers of the ordaining bishop.*

---

*Priests are ordained by bishops only. A bishop possesses the full sacramental authority in the Catholic Church in his own right as bishop. As a bishop, he is a legitimate successor of an Apostle. He receives his powers and his rights as bishop from Jesus himself through the Apostles and the bishops who succeeded the Apostles down through the centuries. The "chief bishop" is the Pope, the bishop of Rome, the successor to St. Peter, the first pope, or leader of the Apostles.

Read the Rite of Ordination on pages 210-213. Answer the following questions on another sheet of paper. Be prepared to discuss your answers with your classmates.

Read Acts 6:1-6. What is the selection about? What action by the Apostles made those selected their official helpers?

What are the special functions of priests in the Catholic Church? What other things do the priests in your parish do?

Select three other religions in your area and find out what their special ministers do.

What is a bishop in the Catholic Church? What is an archbishop? What is a cardinal? Who is the bishop of your diocese?

Are nuns and religious brothers, priests? Why? Why not?

Where does the name "clergy" come from? What does it mean?

During what part of the Mass does the Rite of Ordination take place?

When during the Rite of Ordination do the candidates become priests?

To what Old Testament people does the bishop refer during the Rite of Ordination? Why does he do so?

In Part III of the Rite of Ordination, the bishop asks the person about to be ordained several questions. To what does each refer? How are all the questions related to each other?

At the end of the Rite for Ordination several symbolic actions are given. What does each signify? How are all related to the role of the priest?

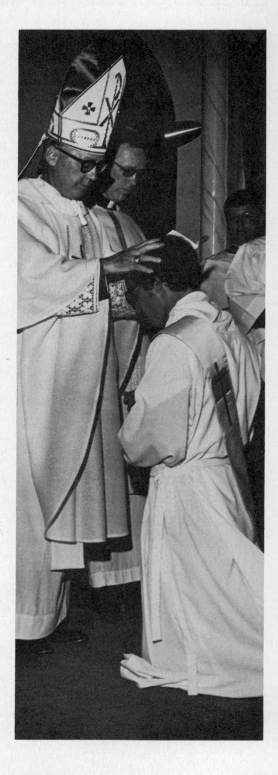

The Rite of Ordination of Several Priests (During Mass)

1. THE INTRODUCTION

The usual introductory rites for Mass take place up to, but not including, the homily, Creed, and Intercessory Prayers (the Prayer of the Faithful).

2. THE CALL TO MINISTRY

Then those to be ordained are called, by name, by the deacon of the Mass: "Let those who are to be ordained come forward." As each one is called, he responds "I am ready and willing," and goes to the bishop where he makes a fitting sign of reverence.

When all are in their places before the bishop, the priest designated by the bishop says:

PRIEST: Most Reverend Father, holy mother Church requests you to ordain our brothers here present for the office of presbyter.

BISHOP: Do you know if they are worthy?

PRIEST: I testify that upon inquiry among the people of God, and upon recommendation of those concerned with their training, they have been found worthy.

BISHOP: We rely on the help of the Lord God and our Savior Jesus Christ and we choose our brothers here present for the office of presbyter.

PEOPLE: *Thanks be to God.*

Then all sit and the bishop addresses the people and the candidates on the duties of a priest.

3. THE RESPONSE TO SERVE

When the bishop has finished his special homily (or instruction), those to be ordained stand facing the bishop. He then presents the following questions.

BISHOP: My sons, before you come forward to be ordained priests you must declare before your people your intention to undertake this office.

Are you resolved, with the help of the Holy Spirit, to discharge without fail the office of priesthood in the rank of presbyters as the trusted partners of the bishops in caring for the Lord's flock?

CANDIDATES: *I am.*

BISHOP: Are you resolved to celebrate the mysteries of Christ faithfully and religiously as the Church has handed them down for the glory of God and the sanctification of Christians?

CANDIDATES: *I am.*

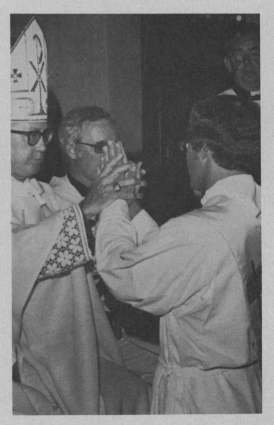

BISHOP: Are you resolved to exercise the ministry of the Word worthily and with wisdom, preaching the gospel and explaining the Catholic faith?

CANDIDATES: *I am.*

BISHOP: Are you resolved to unite yourself more closely every day to Christ the first priest who offered himself for us to the Father as a perfect sacrifice, and to consecrate your life to God for the salvation of men?

CANDIDATES: *I am, with the help of God.*

Then each one of the candidates goes to the bishop and, kneeling before him, places his joined hands between those of the bishop. If this seems less suitable in some places, the episcopal conference may choose another rite.

If the bishop is the candidate's Ordinary, he asks:

BISHOP: Do you promise me and my successors obedience and respect?

CANDIDATE: *I do.* [If the bishop is not the candidate's own Ordinary, he asks:

BISHOP: Do you promise your Ordinary obedience and respect?

CANDIDATE: *I do.*]

BISHOP: May God who began the good work in you bring it to fulfillment.

Then all stand. The bishop faces the people and, with his hands joined, says:

BISHOP: Dearly beloved, let us pray to God the Father all-powerful that he may shower the gifts of heaven on these servants of his, the ones he has chosen for the office of priest.

DEACON: Let us kneel.

After all are kneeling, the litany of the Saints is recited or sung. At its conclusion, the bishop stands and prays aloud.

BISHOP: Listen to us, we pray, Lord our God, and pour out upon these servants of yours the blessing of the Holy Spirit and the strength given to the priesthood. In your sight we offer these men to be set apart for a sacred office. In your unfailing generosity accept our decision, through Christ our Lord.

PEOPLE: *Amen.*

4. THE ORDINATION

After the prayers are concluded, the moment of ordination takes place. One by one the candidates go to the bishop and kneel before him. The bishop lays his hands on the head of each, saying nothing.

Next all the priests present, wearing stoles, lay their hands upon each of the candidates, saying nothing. After the imposition of hands, the priests remain at the sides of the bishop until the prayer of consecration is completed.

When all the candidates for ordination have presented themselves for this "laying on of hands," the bishop says the prayer of consecration.

BISHOP: Come to our aid, O Lord, holy Father, all-powerful eternal God, source of every honor and every office. All growth, all permanence comes from you. Yours is the well-ordered plan by which our personalities unfold to ever greater perfection. In keeping with that plan, you instituted sacred rites to fill the ranks of priests and Levites so that you might designate men as next in rank and dignity to the high priests as associates and helpers of those you had appointed to govern your people. So also in the desert you extended the spirit of Moses by infusing that spirit into the minds of seventy wise men, who were his helpers among the people and whom he employed to govern that great multitude. You filled the sons of Aaron with their father's power, to make them worthy priests for the offering of saving victims and the celebration of sacred rites. By your Providence, Lord, your Son's apostles had companions of second rank, to help them preach the faith to the whole world. We cannot compare with the high priests, with Moses,

Aaron and the apostles. Weaker than they, so much the more are we in need of help. Grant us that help, O Lord.

We ask you, all-powerful Father, give these servants of yours the dignity of the presbyterate. Renew the Spirit of holiness within them. By your divine gift may they attain the second order in the hierarchy and exemplify right conduct in their lives.

May they be our fellow-workers, so that the words of the gospel may reach the farthest parts of the earth, and all nations, gathered together in Christ, may become one holy people of God.

Through Jesus Christ, your Son, our Lord, who lives and reigns with you in the unity of the Holy Spirit, God, forever and ever.

PEOPLE: *Amen.*

Now that the newly ordained are priests, the bishop and the assisting priests "bring them into the community of priests" with several symbolic actions. Among these are the vesting of the newly ordained in the priestly garment of the Eucharistic celebration (the chasuble), anointing the hands of each of the newly ordained with chrism (blessed oil), presenting them with a chalice in which wine and water have been poured, and giving them the appropriate sign of peace.

When all these are done, the Liturgy of the Eucharist is begun. In this liturgy, the newly ordained concelebrate with the bishop as full-fledged ministers of the Eucharistic celebration.

Conclusion

Living in marriage and living in the priesthood are two particular, sacramental ways of living the Christian life. As such, each has special graces and a special kind of relationship with God which enables those living in either vocation to function as a committed Christian giving witness to their social role as married persons or as priests.

Both ways of life build up the human community. The one creates the human potential for growth; the other creates the divine potential. Because of what they are and what they do in the Christian community, they are sacraments in the Catholic Church.

Summary

People are created in God's image. Their dignity and worth are God-given.

Matrimony and Orders are special sacraments. Each has special graces and each creates a special kind of relationship with God.

Matrimony is a sacrament because it is an act of the Church which signifies and causes God's special grace in the lives of two Christians who commit themselves to the sacred union called marriage.

Orders is a sacrament in the Catholic Church which signifies that a person has been selected to function in the sacramental ministry of the Church.

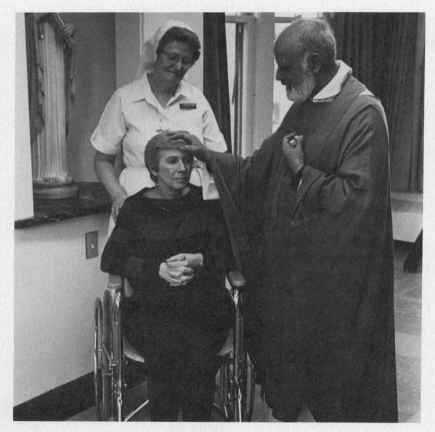

Words You Should Know

Be sure that you know the meaning of the words given below. If you are not sure of any look them up in the Word List on page 234.

✝admonish   ordain   potential
devise   ordinary   transcend
macho   oriented   unique

For Review, Discussion, Research, and Reflection

1. Define both the Sacrament of Matrimony and the Sacrament of Orders. Why are they called "special sacraments"?

2. What do you understand the special grace of the Sacrament of Matrimony to be? Of the Sacrament of Orders?

3. What is marriage a sign of? What is orders a sign of? What is the moment of each sacrament? What is the "continuity" of each? What in matrimony is sacramental?

4. In light of what you now understand about Christian marriage, discuss with your classmates what a Catholic response might be to one who asks why the Church has such strong feelings about premarital sex and abortion.

5. Discuss the ways Christians participate in the priesthood of Christ. (See 1 Corinthians 12:28-30.)

6. How are bishops and priests related to each other in their priesthood? Why is a bishop called "a chief priest"? Of what is he the "chief" priest? How are priests and bishops related to the Pope?

7. Discuss the nature of a "vocation" to the priesthood or the religious life. Do you think that people also have a "vocation" to the married life? Why? Why not?

8. Why does your book refer to the Sacrament of Matrimony and the Sacrament of Orders as creation sacraments?

9. Discuss which is the "better" sacrament, Matrimony or Orders. Be sure to have reasons for your viewpoint.

10. In an encyclopedia or almanac find out how many Catholics there are in the world and how many there are in the United States and Canada. Find out what number the present pope is in the line of popes since St. Peter.

A Celebration Every Week

It is in Christ and through his blood that we have been redeemed and our sins forgiven, so immeasurably generous is God's favor to us. God has given us the wisdom to understand fully the mystery, the plan he was pleased to decree in Christ, to be carried out in the fullness of time: namely, to bring all things in the heavens and on earth into one under Christ's headship.
—Ephesians 1:7–10

8.1 The Liturgical Year

You have noticed, no doubt, that at various times during the year, the priest wears vestments of different colors during the celebration of the Eucharist on Sunday. Sometimes the vestments are white, sometimes red, and sometimes green or purple or gold. You've probably noticed, too, that, if your church uses

"celebration banners" or posters, they, too, change from time to time.

Maybe you know the reason, maybe you don't. There is a reason, of course, and a good one. In its vestment colors, its songs, its words, and its slogans (in addition to the liturgy itself), the Church is proclaiming its remembrance of the salvation acts of Jesus.

The colors, songs, words, and slogans change as the remembrance of the salvation acts changes. The remembrance changes according to what is being celebrated. What is being celebrated is determined by "The Liturgical Calendar." The celebrations laid out in the Liturgical Calendar make up "The Liturgical Year" or, as it is sometimes called, "The Church Year."

The Liturgical or Church Year is a calendar year considered from the standpoint of what is being celebrated in the weekly (that is, Sunday) liturgy. It is a year-long calendar of liturgical celebrations through which the Catholic Church recalls and celebrates the "Mystery of Christ."* That is to say, the Catholic Church, officially in its Sunday liturgy celebrates the coming of Jesus into the world of people, the salvational events in the life of Jesus, and the meaning of those events in the world.

---

*As you know, in Catholic terminology, the word *mystery* means God's revelation of Himself. Hence "Mystery of Christ" means God's revelation of Himself in Christ—what God revealed of Himself through the birth, life, death and resurrection of Jesus and his life in the Church. In a similar manner, "the mystery of creation" is God's revelation of Himself in creation.

It must be clearly understood, however, that the liturgy of the Catholic Church does not simply recall and celebrate a past event—as important as this is. It recalls and celebrates a present reality: God acting in and through Jesus in the world at the present time in the life of the Church. life of.

The reason for this is at once simple but deeply theological. As you know, Christians believe that Jesus is the Son of God or, as we say, is God expressing Himself humanly. They believe that God actually became a real human person and lived as a real human being. They believe that they actually come into contact with God in Jesus. Because of this, they believe that for them, God is no longer just "out there." He is no longer utterly remote—to be acknowledged as God but totally beyond people's capacity to experience except indirectly in His creation or in their own thoughts or in their own theories. They believe that they can experience God in person in Jesus. They believe that they can experience God as they experience other human persons—in what is called interpersonal relationships. *This is the meaning of the sacraments, which, as we said, are encounters with Christ.*

This God-entering-His-creation-in-the-person-of-Jesus belief unlocks a whole theology of God that affects the thinking of Catholics in their relationship with God. It is what makes Christianity so radically different from other religions.*

---

*You will recall that we have said elsewhere that one definition of religion is that it is the attempt on the part of people to express their relationship with whatever God is for them.

First of all, the very thought of God becoming a real human person is, on the surface, completely beyond expectation. It is not something people could hope for, expect, demand, pray, or long for because it is, they think, not "God-like." Philosophically speaking, how could God be God and man? Practically speaking, from a human viewpoint, it is impossible. Yet, Christians believe it is so. And why not? Is anything impossible to God? Yet, only God could do it—only He could do the "impossible."

Secondly, this God-as-human-person belief changes the idea that human beings are limited to time—unable to attain their ideals, and condemned to oblivion forever. Because God has become a man, people are saved from a nondivine existence. Because God shares His life with them, they are made capable of attaining their ideals, and are saved from oblivion. They can look forward to a fuller share in God's life in their own risen life when they enter the life-dimension of eternity.

Thirdly, because Jesus lives (this is the meaning of the resurrection), he is present to people now, enabling them to encounter God in the person of Jesus, who expresses himself in and through the Church in the liturgical actions of the Church.

So the Church celebrates this Mystery of Christ because it is something worth celebrating. Each "season" of the Church year, the Church celebrates a major salvational act of Jesus on a progressive basis. Each Sunday of a particular season, an aspect of that salvation act is recalled and celebrated. By the end of each liturgical year, all the major saving acts of Jesus are recalled, made present, and celebrated. As you know, this is what the liturgy is—and is for.

Find out what vestments a priest wears when celebrating the Eucharist. Be able to name them.

On a sheet of paper, make a working model for a celebration banner for your church. On another sheet, make one for a Mass your class might celebrate at this time of year.

If you have a Liturgical Calendar at home, look up today's date. What is being celebrated in the liturgy?

The next time you go to Mass, or drop in at your church, spend a few minutes looking at and thinking about the celebration banners in your church.

Be sure that you can explain what "salvation acts of Jesus" means.

What do "recalls, makes present, and celebrates" mean as far as the liturgy is concerned?

8.2 The Liturgical Calendar

The Liturgical Year, like the calendar year, contains seasons, periods, feast days, and special events. Just as the calendar year is divided into seasons which mark the major divisions of the year (spring, summer, fall, and winter), so does the Liturgical Year have its seasons. Just as the calendar year contains periods (the growth of spring, the ripening of summer, the decline of fall, and the sleep of winter), so does the Liturgical Year have periods. Just as the calendar year contains remembrances of important events and names (the Fourth of July, Lincoln's birthday), so does the Liturgical Year.

The feast of Christmas, for example, celebrates the birth of Jesus. The Christmas season celebrates the saving presence of Jesus in the world. Easter celebrates, as you know, the resurrection of Jesus. The Easter season celebrates the risen life of Jesus in his Church. Each Sunday in the season, as we said, celebrates a particular aspect of that season. It is the days

"I am from above."–John 8:21

221

and times of the feasts, seasons, periods, and events recalled that make up the Liturgical Calendar.

The Liturgical Calendar begins four Sundays before Christmas and continues for 52 weeks celebrating each Sunday, in a progressive fashion, the saving events in the life of Jesus.

We do not have time, of course, to discuss the entire Liturgical Calendar in detail. There are certain things about the Church calendar, however, which, if they are understood, make sense out of the

entire Church year. Among these things are the following.

A. The Development of the Church Year. The calendar of the Church as we now have it was a product of gradual growth. The first Christians recalled the resurrection of Jesus (the central event in their minds) on the first day of each week. They celebrated it with Jesus' own memorial—the primitive Eucharist in which they recalled his own action of the Last Supper. Each year they celebrated with a special remembrance the day of his resurrection which coincided with the

"I am Come forth from the Father."—John 16:28

222

beginning of their own Jewish Passover. (Jesus was, for them, the Passover Lamb.)

As time went on, other major events in the life of Jesus were recalled and celebrated and the calendar grew. Eventually, the major events in the life of Jesus were recalled and celebrated in the Eucharist. Each year these events were repeated in celebration. Eventually the Church, after many centuries, had what became known as the "Jesus cycle"—the repetition of the celebration of the major events in the life of Jesus in a regular pattern.

B. The Celebration of the Event. As each event is recalled and celebrated, the event itself is recalled in the theme of the Mass and in the readings, hymns, prayers, and responses of the Mass. It is celebrated in the Eucharist in which Jesus is made present in his body and blood.

C. The Centrality of Easter. As important as all the events of the life of Jesus are for Christians, the most important one, and the one that makes sense of all

"I am the Resurrection and the Life."–John 11:25

the others, is the Easter event—the resurrection of Jesus.

The experience of Jesus alive after his very real death gave meaning and purpose to the experience the first Christians had had of Jesus as a man. It put everything he had said and done in a new light. It gave them a new perspective about the meaning of Jesus for humanity. It, as it were, "made" Jesus for them. It told them something about Jesus that they would not have known if he had not risen. It made complete sense out of their expectation of a Jewish Messiah. It is no wonder they celebrated the Easter event when they came together on the day he arose: the first day of the week.

Today, the Church continues to celebrate the Easter event on Sundays for the same reasons. And for the same reasons, it continues to be the most important saving event in the life of Jesus celebrated in the liturgy.

D. The Structure of the Church Year. The regular pattern of celebration of the Jesus cycle (or the yearly unfolding of the Mystery of Christ) contains five principal parts or seasons: Advent, Christmas, Lent, Easter, and Pentecost.

8.3 The Seasons of the Church Year Explained

As we mentioned above, each season of the Church Year forms a part of the year-long celebration of the Mystery of Christ. Each one commemorates a specific major event in the unfolding process of God's plan of salvation-in-Christ. It celebrates its present reality in the lives of Christians. Within each season, feasts which enlarge on the salvation event of the season are celebrated, like the feast of the Immaculate Conception which occurs during the Advent season.

As we said, the Church Year begins with the Season of Advent—four Sundays before Christmas. During these weeks, the Church prepares for the celebration of the birth of Jesus by the presenting in the theme of the Mass, in the Liturgy of the Word, and in the prayers, hymns, and responses, the expectation of the Messiah. But the expectation presented by the Church is not simply the expectation of the past. It is the expectation of the present coming of Jesus into the lives of people and the establishment of the kingdom of God as a reality in the present and in the unknown future (called "the Second Coming" of Jesus).

The Season of Advent, then, is a celebration of the past, the present, and the future. As a celebration of the past, it affords Catholic Christians an opportunity to thank God for sending His Son into the world (an event of past history), for making him present to all in this moment of history, and for the anticipated fulfillment of the mission of Jesus when God's kingdom will be established at the end of earth-time.

The yearly repetition of the celebration of the past, present, and future coming of Jesus is also a sign that the actions of Jesus in the past, present, and future are a reality in the world of people.

From December 25 to the beginning of Lent—during the **Christmas Season**— the Church celebrates the birth of Jesus. But the celebration is not confined to the

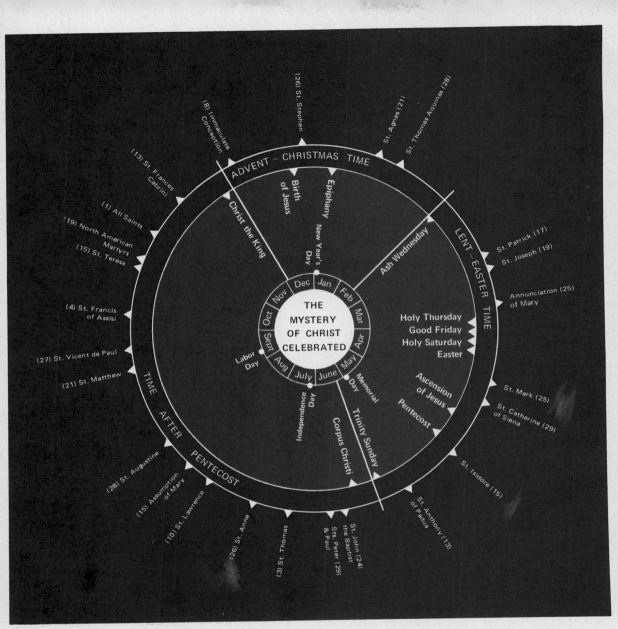

past event of Jesus' being born in Bethlehem. It is a celebration of the manifestation of Jesus to the world. After all, that is what the birth of Jesus really was—his becoming visibly present to the world. By recalling not only the events of his birth, but also the various ways in which Jesus became known to others, the Church in her liturgy celebrates his continual manifestation of himself to people through the centuries. Like Advent, Christmas is also a sign. It is a sign of Jesus present among his people acting in the world in the present time.

The third season of the Church Year is the **Lenten Season.** Forty-six days before Easter the Church begins its celebration by recalling the events which led up to Easter and made the resurrection of

Jesus a possibility. It presents the trials, the confrontations, the disappointments, and the drama of events which resulted in the sufferings and death of Jesus. But the recollection of the events and the liturgical celebration are not a celebration of suffering. *They are a celebration of the triumph of Jesus over suffering and death.*

Through the themes of the Lenten Masses, and in the Liturgy of the Word, the prayers, hymns, and responses of each Lenten Mass, the Church recalls the trials and sufferings of Jesus. In so doing, the Church reminds us of the limitation of human endeavor, the need for overcoming the evil in the world, and the importance of looking forward to overcoming the trials and sufferings of life in the reality of our own resurrection. In this sense, Lent is a sign to the world that evil is overcome through the courageous action of people who try to do something about it in their own lives and in the world they immediately affect.

On Easter Sunday, the Church begins its **Easter Season.** As we have said, the Easter event is the most important event celebrated in the Church Year. Because of its close relationship with the Jewish Passover, it is celebrated in the springtime (in northern latitude countries) when the Jewish Passover is celebrated by the Jewish people. From time to time, the Jewish Passover and Christian Easter may not exactly coincide due to small differences in calendars, but Christians celebrate Easter on the first Sunday after the first full moon of springtime—that is, sometime between March 22 and April 25.

The celebration of Easter, however, is not only a celebration of a past event. It is a celebration of a present reality and a future hope: the presence of the risen Jesus in his Church and the anticipation of a risen life after earthly death for all people.

Because of what it recalls and what it celebrates, the Easter season is a season of joy and a sign of hope. It lasts until Pentecost (50 days) and the themes of the Masses of Easter, the Liturgy of the Word, and the prayers, responses, and hymns all deal with the experiences of the Apostles of the risen Jesus.

From Pentecost Sunday to the first Sunday of Advent the Church celebrates the day and the meaning of the coming of the Holy Spirit to the Church. This is the **Pentecost Season.**

As you know, the feast of Pentecost recalls and celebrates the coming of the Holy Spirit to the Apostles (Acts 2) and the beginning of "the Christian era." But as with other liturgical celebrations, the celebration of Pentecost is not simply the recalling and celebrating of a past event. It celebrates a present reality: the presence of the Spirit in the world, and the mission of the Church to make real the kingdom of God which Jesus came to establish. As a yearly celebration it, too, is a sign. It is a sign of God's action in the affairs of the world through the activity of Christians, who are called to be Christ to the world.

For some twenty-plus Sundays, the Church in her liturgy, by recalling how Jesus acted in his mission, reminds Christians how they are to act as Christ in the world. On the last Sunday of the Pentecost Season, the Church reminds Christians of the end of time when Jesus will return to bring his people in triumph to the Father. In this way, the Church closes its liturgical year with a reference to what is celebrated, by anticipation, in Advent. Then the whole cycle begins again—a new Liturgical Year begins.

See what you can find out about the origin of calendars. What calendar do people in the United States use?

What determines the seasons of the year?

Why is Easter always in the springtime in northern latitude countries? When is it celebrated in South America? When is Christmas celebrated?

Read the Gospel accounts of the Resurrection. Be ready to say who discovered that Jesus' body was missing. How did the Apostles know that Jesus was alive and that his body had not just been stolen? Give three examples of how Jesus appeared to his Apostles after his resurrection.

Using any Sunday Mass text you wish, show how the theme of that Mass is carried out in the readings, songs, and prayers.

feasts of saints celebrated on days other than Sunday or the other feasts of Jesus.

These feasts are celebrated to recall the triumph of Christ in the lives of particular persons whom the Church has canonized (or put on its official list of saints), like Mary the Mother of Jesus, St. Elizabeth Seton, St. Thomas More, and St. John de la Salle. Because of the special expression of Jesus in their lives, the saints are a sign to other Christians that they are called to holiness and can attain that holiness.

It is significant that the Church traditionally celebrates the triumph of Christ in the saints, not on the day of their birth into the world, but on the day of their "birth" into eternity—usually the day the person died (for example, the martyrs). The Church, however, does not celebrate the death, the trials, or the achievements of the saints. *It celebrates the action of God in their lives.* In the theme of the Mass, in the Liturgy of the Word, in the prayers, hymns, and responses, the Church recalls with thanks, the activity of God as that activity was manifested in a particular way in the life of the person whose feast day it is. For example, the feasts of Mary celebrate in one way or another her Motherhood of Jesus. The feasts of the Apostles celebrate the action of God in His special missionaries of Christ. The feasts of the saintly popes celebrate the holiness of these popes, and so on.

Throughout the year, the Church celebrates feasts of the saints on weekdays. Sundays, in more ways than one, are "the Lord's Day." We celebrate the saving actions of Jesus each Sunday. This is why we go to Mass.

8.4 Other Feasts in the Liturgical Calendar

Because the Church Year and the Liturgical Calendar are Christ-centered, special days, and particular feasts like Corpus Christi or the Trinity, are celebrated because they are closely related to the Jesus cycle of feasts and seasons.

In addition to celebrating these special feasts related to Jesus, the Church also celebrates what is known as the **Sanctoral Cycle.** The sanctoral cycle is the

The Sundays of the Church Year and the special feasts of Jesus and certain saints make up the Liturgical Calendar. Every week there is a celebration of the saving acts of Jesus. Every day there is a remembrance of those saving acts as they were manifested in the life of some saint.

What do you suppose happens to the feast of a saint that happens to fall on a Sunday?

When is the feast day of your patron saint? For what was he or she known?

When is the feast of the patron of your school and your church? For what is each known? During what season of the Church Year are these feasts celebrated?

During what part of the Creed do we profess our faith in the triumph of the saints? What does that phrase mean?

Take some time to study the calendar chart on page 225. Note when the major seasons occur, when the important feasts of Jesus are, and when the feast of the Immaculate Conception is. Why is the feast of the Immaculate Conception an important feast in the United States?

In an almanac or Catholic dictionary see if you can find a list of saints by what they are patrons of. Pick out ten who interest you.

Conclusion

For the Christian who appreciates the meaning of the Church calendar, the Church Year can be a "year of grace" and a year of growth in Christ. It can be a year of grace because God manifests Himself and makes Himself present in

Christ in a special way in the liturgy to those who are open to His manifestation. It can be a year of growth in Christ because through active participation in the Christ cycle, a person becomes more acquainted with Jesus and grows in knowledge of him. He or she is also inevitably drawn closer to him, participates with him in his actions, and shares the grace grace that Jesus offers to him in the liturgical life of the Church.

Although the Catholic Church is the body of Christ, it becomes the visible body of Christ most surely in its liturgy. It is there that the Risen Jesus makes himself immediately available to those who believe in him. This is the whole purpose and meaning of the Catholic liturgy.

Summary

The Catholic Church celebrates a different aspects of the Mystery of Christ every Sunday.

The celebration is determined by the Liturgical Year and the Liturgical Calendar.

The saints are also remembered in Eucharistic celebrations because they have shown in their lives effects of God's grace on those who have cooperated fully with the special graces He gives each one.

Words You Should Know

Be sure that you can define the words given below. If there are any you are not sure of, look them up in the Word List on page 234.

coincide	oblivion	perspective
manifestation	paschal	sanctoral
nondivine	Pentecost	terminology

For Review, Discussion, Research, and Reflection

1. According to your book, what makes Christianity so different from other religions?

2. What do you understand by the phrase "Mystery of Christ"? What does "the salvation acts of Jesus" mean to you?

3. In your own words explain what is meant by the Liturgical Year, by the Liturgical Calendar, by Jesus cycle, and by sanctoral cycle.

4. Name and explain the seasons of the Church Year.

5. What do the priest's vestments, the colors, the songs, and the banners tell you about a particular liturgy? Give an example.

6. Why is Easter the central feast of the Church Year? Why do Catholic Christians think that Easter is the most important event in the Christ event?

7. Why do Catholics go to Mass on Sunday?

8. Reread the Psalm that was quoted on page v of your book. Think about it in light of what you know about the liturgy, then use it as a prayer of thanksgiving to God for His kindness to you.

Worship begins within.
It springs from the intellect and
the will, the spiritual parts of man.
It must, however, at the same time
express itself externally in that body
which is the inseparable companion
of the soul.

William O'Shea

A Conclusion

Now that you have thought about, discussed, and come to a deeper understanding of Christian worship, you have come to realize that prayer—in any of its expressions—is not a duty to be performed reluctantly, but a response to the Mystery of God-in-Christ. You have learned that liturgical prayer is your faith-community's official Church-response to what the Mystery of Christ is for your Church. You have learned that this official response is not a series of empty rituals, watched or endured, as the case may be. It is the visible means that God uses to enable you to encounter Christ in his Church, the Body of Christ.

There is only one question that remains for you to consider at this stage of your consideration of Christian worship and that is: What does this mean for you?

Obviously, it means that you are now able to participate more meaningfully in the liturgy. But it means much more than that. It means that you can be a sacrament of Christ—a sign and a reality selected by Christ to be his means for others to encounter him. Through your private prayer life, through your expressing in your relationships with others the Jesus-principle of love, and through your mature participation in the official worship that the Church offers to God, you can become a living symbol and a positive reality of what Christ is for the world: a redeeming force. You can be what you are called to be as a Christian—Christ to the world that does not know him.

As you know, the purpose of Christ's coming was not simply to appear on earth, to live for a brief time among people doing good works and saying "proper" things. *It was to establish God's kingdom on earth*. He came to impregnate creation with the Divine Life, to help people know God for what He is, to give people a means to encounter God in the reality of their lives, to teach people what it means to be human, and to enable them to live as *God's* people. He did all of these things during his earthly life, and he continues to do them in his risen life through his sacrament, his Church.

The mission to the Church in the world, therefore, is the mission of Christ—to preach the kingdom of God, to bring Christ to all people, to afford them an opportunity to encounter Christ, to establish the peace of Christ—(the kingdom of God) on earth. In other words, the mission of the Church is to be Christ to the world. But you are the Church! It is up to you to be Christ to the world. It is up to you to live in such a way that your life reflects what you believe life is and leads others to realize, as you do that

To Live Is Christ!

Word List

admonish—to warn; to rebuke; to find fault with

adversely—unfortunately; affect badly

affirmation—agreement; to give assent to

anoint—to rub or mark with oil; to designate a favorite

assimilate—to make part of the system; to take in

baptismal font—the place where baptismal water is kept in a church; literally, a fountain for baptism

beatification—process of declaring a person beatified or in the second step toward canonization

canonization—the process in which a person is officially declared a saint in the Catholic Church

catechism—a book containing the fundamental beliefs of a particular religion, usually stated in question and answer form

catechumens—learners in the early Christian Church; a beginner; one not admitted to the sacraments

coincide—to be at the same time; together; alike

compassionate—sympathetic; giving help in sorrow or pain; showing pity, mercy, or concern

compel—force

complex process—difficult way of doing; complicated

contemplative—one who thinks seriously about things, especially one who devotes his or her life to thinking about God and the things of God

context—within the framework of; closely related to and receiving its particular meaning from the words, phrases and ideas among which it is found

covenant—solemn agreement; formal, ritualized agreement between God and the partner to the covenant

cultural—referring to culture or the overall way of life of a society

decorum—behaving with good manners; acting with reserve and in accord with good taste

default—failure to appear; neglect

dynamics of growth—the energy and forces involved in growth

economics—the monetary aspects of life

efficacy—worth

Father of the Church—an important scholar, writer, speaker, or teacher in the first 600 years of the Christian Church who had great influence on succeeding generations of teachers and thinkers in the Church

form (in sacramental liturgy)—the words and/or gestures used

frivolous—not serious; giddy; not important

global—universal; pertaining to all people in the world

holiness—degree of relationship with whatever God is

homage—honor; giving signs of submission to someone considered of greater station or importance

homily—the address given by a priest, cleric, or appointed person on the contents of the Gospel message read at a particular liturgy; a sermon given at Mass

hypocrite—one who deceives by acting or speaking about things he does not believe in or ordinarily does just to look good; one who is not sincere; pretending what one is not

hypotenuse—the line in a triangle opposite the right angle

immanent—close at hand; about to happen; close

impact—effect

incomprehensible—cannot be known; not understandable

indiscriminate—not in order; without plan

inherent—a very part of; belonging to the nature of

interacting—one thing influencing another

integrate—necessary part of; real

leper—one suffering from a disfiguring skin disease; an outcast

liturgy—the official, public worship or act of the Church

macho—excessive display of one's maleness; acting as if women are inferior by nature

manifestation—a showing; making visible

matter (in regard to the sacraments)—the material used

memorialize—to remember or recall a person or an event in a solemn way; to commemorate

nondivine—without the divine; outside of God; without God as immanent

oblivion—forgotten; put out of mind; not remembered

ordain—to make official; to designate or appoint

Ordinary (as used in the Catholic Church)—the bishop of a diocese

orient—to determine the position of; to adjust in relation to; to familiarize

Paraclete—a word used to designate the Third Person of the Trinity in Christian theology

paraliturgical—like liturgy; similar to but not the same as liturgy

Paschal—referring to Easter

Passover—Jewish feast commemorating the exodus from Egypt especially the events of the final night before departure

penitent—one who is sorrowful; one who has confessed sins and is doing penance

Pentecost—a Christian feast celebrating the coming of the Holy Spirit fifty days after Easter

perspective—putting things in proper relationship to each other

philosophical—thoughtful; associated with philosophy

plaguing—bothering constantly or severely

political—relating to the art of governing; having a reason based on position or politics

potential—capability; possible; probable

prelude—before; that which comes before the main thing

priorities—order of importance

realm—area; region; kingdom

reconciliation—to bring back; to accept again; to renew

relatively—not exactly; nearly

religiosity—religious actions done hypocritically or for show

ritual—the way things should be done; a set form for doing things; the actions prescribed for the liturgy

sacramental—pertaining to the sacraments; holy

sanctoral—referring to the saints

scrupulous—overly serious; worried, especially about religious things

shoddy—poor; unkempt; without care

social dimension—as it relates to society or to the relationships of people

sophisticated—not simple; characterized by tastes cultivated through education; acting with class

specific—exact; certain

spontaneous—immediate; without plan

stagnate—cease growing; lacking life or energy

technology—that which deals with industry, machines, and tools

tenor—a course of thought or meaning or action that characterizes something

terminology—words used in a particular branch of knowledge

transcendent—beyond, past the material world; outside of; to be above and outside of

uniqueness—single in kind; exceptional

vacillate—to change constantly; not secure or fastened down; changeable

vandalism—the act of useless destruction; destroying for no reason or out of spite

variables—things that change

verbalize—to put into words; to express vocally

wary—cautiously; acting with care and hesitation; careful

Western civilization—the civilization found in countries influenced by early Greek philosophy; the countries of Western Europe, North America, and those influenced by them.

INDEX

Monotheism
   development of, 19
Moses, 21
Mystery of Christ
   celebrated, 220, 225
   meaning of, 219–220
"Mystery of Creation," 219
Mystery of life, v.

N

Nuns (see Religious Life)

O

Orders (Sacrament of)
   matter and form of, 208
   Rite of Ordination, 210–212
   role of bishop in, 209
   role of the community in, 209

P

Paraclete (see Holy Spirit)
Passover
   celebrated in liturgy, 223
Pastor
   role of, 208
Pentecost
   feast of, 227
   season of, 226
Philosophy of life
   development of, 7
Poor Clare Nuns, 60
Pope
   as "chief bishop," 209
   role of, 209
Prayer
   Christian prayer, 27
   difficulty with, 26
   as expression of faith, 69
   God's answer to, 81–82
   group prayer, 91
   liturgical prayer, 91
   The Lord's, 33
   mental, 75

moments of, 70
personal, 78
prayer-life, 25–29
private prayer, 98
public prayer, 98–99
relationship of trust to, 82
as response, 27, 32
ritual, 80
special forms of, 75
types of, 71
Priesthood (see also Holy Orders)
   of the faithful, 207
   function of, 207
   "orders" of, 208
   sacramental ministry of, 208
Priests, 58

R

Reconciliation (Sacrament of)
   communal, 172
   Communal Rite of, 177–179
   essence of, 171
   "healing sacrament," 169
   Individual Rite of, 175
   matter and form of, 172
   meaning of, 171
   necessary elements of, 173–174
   private, 172
   role of community in, 172
   role of priest in, 172
Religious faith
   development of, v.
Religious life
   in community, 59
   description of, 59
   emphasis of, 59
   as sign, 61
Religious orders
   contemplative, 60
   missionary, 60
Resurrection
   celebrated in liturgy, 220, 222–224
   centrality of, 223–224
   meaning of, 23, 92